Nevada

Nevada

A Bicentennial History

Robert Laxalt

University of Nevada Press

Reno / Las Vegas

Nevada: A Bicentennial History was originally published by W. W. Norton & Company, Inc., and the American Association for State and Local History in 1977. The costs of writing and editing were met mainly by grants from the National Endowment for the Humanities, a federal agency. The project was administered by the American Association for State and Local History, a non-profit learned society, under the general editorship of James Morton Smith, general editor, and Gerald George, managing editor. The present volume reproduces the original edition except for the following changes: the front matter has been modified to reflect the new publisher, a new preface has been added, and minior alterations have been made in the text.

Cover design by Carrie House.

Library of Congress Cataloging-in-Publication Data

Laxalt, Robert, 1923–2001
Nevada : a bicentennial history / Robert Laxalt.
   p.   cm.
Originally published: New York : Norton, 1977, in series:
The States and the National series. With new pref.
Includes bibliographical references and index.
ISBN 0-87417-179-2 (paperback ed. : alk. paper)
1. Nevada—History. I. Title
F841.L39 1991   91-31281
979.3—dc20

University of Nevada Press, Reno, Nevada 89557 USA

The paper used in this book meets the requirements of American
National Standard for Information Sciences—Permanence of Paper
for Printed Library Materials, ANSI/NISO Z39.48-1992 (R2002).
Binding materials were selected for strength and durability.

This book has been reproduced as a digital reprint.

ISBN 13: 978-0-87417-179-2

For
Gabriel, Amy,
Alexandra, and Kevin—
the next generation.

Contents

Illustrations

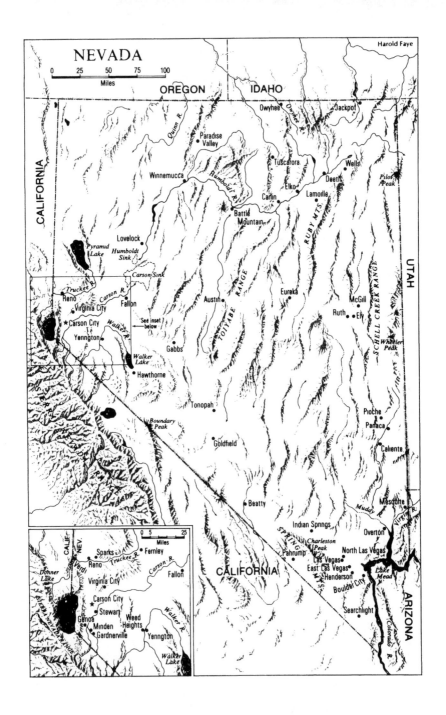

Preface to the New Edition

A decade has come and gone since *Nevada: A History* was first penned. It was written at the time of the bicentennial of the American Revolution, which was also memorialized by other state histories in the States and the Nation Series. Publishers were W. W. Norton, Inc., of New York, and the American Association for State and Local History.

The thrust of the series was unusual, but it was one to warm the heart of any author. Instead of a laborious chronicling of events, each book was to be "a summing up—interpretive, sensitive, thoughtful, individual, even personal—of what seems significant about a state's history."

The authors were thus allowed the delightful liberty of judging what was important enough to be included in their states' histories. Not only that, they were unshackled to speak from their hearts as well as their minds. This does not happen often in the writing of history.

I suspect that not many writers go back to read what they wrote ten years ago. More of them should, as I did, duty bound by the fact of a reprinting of this book. The act forces us to judge the past anew, and more importantly, to test the validity of our earlier projections for the future. What naturally follows is the question: "What of lasting importance has happened in my state in the last decade?"

In the original edition, I had predicted "economic soundness and quality of life" in the Nevada of the future. The first prediction held true. The second did not, at least in the metropolitan areas surrounding Las Vegas and Reno.

If anything, Nevada has a sounder economic base today than then. State government is healthy, even without imposing taxes on income, inheritance, corporate presence, and goods-in-transit.

Gambling is still the state's major industry and the income from the accompanying tourism continues to grow. For example, fifteen million tourists a year now visit Las Vegas. The world's largest hotel, the Excalibur, has 3,500 rooms. The Mirage is not far behind with 3,000 rooms, and Bally's, formerly the MGM Grand, is aiming for 5,000 rooms. Nearby on the Colorado River, in a setting of furnace heat, the town of Laughlin is a modern-day gambling phenomenon.

Industrialist and mystery magnate Howard Hughes died in 1976, leaving as a legacy a hotel-casino empire purged of the Mafia presence that had once corrupted Las Vegas.

The glittering roster of entertainers that dominated Nevada showrooms in the 1980s has dwindled. Death claimed such figures of legend as Elvis Presley, Sammy Davis, Jr., Pearl Bailey, and Liberace. Frank Sinatra and Bill Cosby remain—and we can leave it to Las Vegas to come up with innovative ideas to fill the gaps.

Today, "the showroom is the hotel itself," as one former entertainment writer put it. The Mirage hotel with its spewing volcanoes and "real live" dolphins and tigers is the epitome of an adult Disneyland that transports tourists to exotic realms.

In a state whose beginnings were founded on rich silver strikes, gold has become the principal mining venture—not the veins and pockets of glory, but microscopic gold found in low-yield ore mined with massive machinery in yawning open pits. A dozen of these operations in the remote areas of Nevada have made us the biggest gold producer in the United States.

Nevada's forever vastnesses continue to lure nuclear and defense projects. The Nevada Test Site still detonates nuclear devices underground in southern Nevada. Nellis Air Force Base nearby is the training center for the newest in fighter planes. Gunnery and bombing ranges consume desolate deserts.

But enough is enough. When it came to making Nevada the home of the MX missile, public protest was so pronounced that President Ronald Reagan vetoed the military. The same coalition has regrouped to oppose formation of a nuclear waste depository deep underground at Yucca Mountain a hundred miles northwest of Las Vegas. The nuclear waste to be buried there has an active life of ten thousand years. No more need be said.

Other things of lasting value also came about in the 1980s. One was the creation of Great Basin National Park in eastern Nevada—a pristine expanse of 76,800 acres of mountain and desert.

On the political front, Robert List, Richard Bryan, and Bob Miller joined the roster of Nevada governors. Bryan went on to become U.S. senator, as did Harry Reid, former lieutenant governor. James Santini concluded four terms in the House of Representatives; Barbara Vucanovich and James Bilbray now serve in the Congress. Incumbent senator Howard Cannon was defeated after long tenure, and former governor Paul Laxalt went on to serve two six-year terms in the U.S. Senate. Before retiring from politics, Laxalt became the first Nevadan ever to run for president of the United States. The move was audacious but hopeless, and Laxalt withdrew. It may be a long time before another candidate from Nevada runs for the presidency.

As if making up for its unenviable record from the early days of women's rights, the 1980s saw two historic breakthroughs. Frankie Sue Del Papa became the first woman elected secretary of state. Not stopping there, she went on to become the first woman attorney general of Nevada. The frosting on the cake of feminine presence in government came when Sue Wagner became the first woman elected lieutenant governor.

Since the original publication of *Nevada: A History,* time has taken its toll of some of the Nevadans I most admired: Dr. Mary Fulstone, who in her lifetime delivered more than four thousand babies in two farming and ranching valleys surrounding the hamlet of Yerington in western Nevada; Jesusa Saval, the valiant Basque woman who donned jeans and boots and spurs when her husband was killed, and "ramrodded" a major cattle outfit in central Nevada; Anthony Amaral, biographer of cowboy author-artist Will James and my companion on mustang searches, who died as he wanted to—fighting down a stallion at the end of a rope; Rose Walter, the venerable guardian of stone ruins and tumbledown shacks in the ghost town of Belmont, "because they belong to someone somewhere." (There is little or no vandalism to this day in Belmont. I like to think Rose Walter's shade protects the ruins still.)

In the years I was growing up in Nevada, nearly everyone seemed to be waiting with bated breath for the state to reach the nirvana of one million population. It has happened now; the 1990 census officially pronounced that 1,280,020 people live in Nevada. There were no celebrations when it happened. Nevadans recoiled at the price they were paying for too many people. Las Vegas and Reno in particular were stunned as all the ills of overcrowded cities descended upon them like the plague: air pollution, traffic jams, overflowing schools, murder and burglary and rape, gangs, and a devastating shortage of water.

My prophecy regarding "quality of life" no longer applies to once stately Reno with its San Francisco elegance or to that brash upstart of a town called Las Vegas.

Only the small towns of Nevada—scattered over an unbelievable reach of land—have escaped the fate of Las Vegas and Reno. It is there I must go now to find what is left of the Nevada I knew.

With the blue Nevada sky wrapping me around, I can still stand on peaks where it is possible to look for a hundred miles without any signs of habitation, range upon range of desert mountains in hues of rose, gray, and purple following one upon the other into the interminable distance.

Robert Laxalt

March 1991

Preface

IN the writing of this book, I have departed—perhaps radically—from the conventional approaches to history. I really cannot explain why, except to say that it was right for me. I do not pretend to be a scholarly historian. In that, I must defer to the meticulous and definitive histories of such as Dr. Russell Elliott, Dr. Wilbur Shepperson, Dr. Eleanore Bushnell, Dr. James Hulse of the University of Nevada faculty at Reno, and the historians who went before them.

But I do pretend to know the Nevada in which I was reared and where it is possible to have intimate exposures to the diverse facets of its makeup—from range life to mining towns to the gambling scene and to politics.

Out of these exposures, I have attempted to shape a narrative history of my state as I have seen it and as I have learned about it. The reader will find no footnotes here, simply because they are to me obtrusive in a narrative treatment. Neither will he find an abundance of dates and statistics, which should properly be contained in the more formalized histories.

The reader will find, however, liberal use of the language of the people, sometimes to introduce a chapter and sometimes to end it. This I have done purposely and also may be construed as unconventional.

But to me, nothing is more revealing of the character, attitudes, and environment of a region than the pure language of the people who inhabit it. Their expression needs no broadening upon. It speaks for itself in the said and the unsaid.

ROBERT LAXALT

Nevada

1

Lesson of the Land

$\mathcal{U}$NTIL the letter caught up with me, I had taken Nevada pretty much for granted. I suppose that attitude was a normal one for youth who have known only one setting from the time of first awareness until the circumstance of war catapults them across a continent and an ocean and deposits them in an alien land.

So it was with me. The letter was from a friend in Nevada. That much I noticed. But I was only vaguely aware that there seemed to be something more than paper inside. When I was alone, I opened the envelope. With the unsealing came the unleashing of a forgotten scent that struck me like a physical force.

Hidden between the pages was a single sprig of Nevada sagebrush. Before I could protect myself, the memories were summoned up and washed over me in a flood. They all had to do with sagebrush.

Sagebrush that rolled over the vast plateaus and brutal desert mountains like an endless gray sea, ringing the few scattered hamlets and towns of Nevada so that they were like islands in that sea. Sagebrush growing down to the banks of rare streams and rivers so that water seemed to be captive in a bigger sea. Sagebrush giving up its domain only when it reached the foothills of the western Sierra where deep forests of pine and fir and tamarack ruled supreme.

3

Sagebrush in the spring with the tender tips of first growth mingling with the gray. Sagebrush in the summer when the blazing sun made the scent almost unbearably pungent. Sagebrush after a spring rain when that scent was muted to the heady fragrance of wine. Sagebrush in the autumn when golden pods burst into puffs at the mere touch of a hand. Sagebrush in the winter, hooded white with snow so that walking through it was like walking through a gnome forest.

The smell of a sagebrush cookfire at dusk in a desert hollow that was bedground for our sheep, shaggy sheepdogs resting in its light and warmth, and the indistinct figure of my father saying that sagebrush made the hottest cookfire one could ask for. A tobacco-chewing prospector with a stained mouth and a face so scarred by sun and wind that his wrinkles were like black ravines in his flesh, stopping by for coffee out of a blackened pot, while his overloaded burro waited with hanging head until he could be relieved of a burden made impossible by a hundred pieces of promising rock. A buckaroo with a big hat and built-up heels on his way home to the ranch at end of day, his powerful horse plowing through the sagebrush as if it were an enemy. The Paiute Indian boys of my childhood running with fluid motion through an unbroken tangle of sagebrush without even breaking their stride, because sagebrush was in their blood and bones, and their familiarity with it was drawn down from uncounted generations who had hunted there before the first white man had dared venture into the unknown land.

Since that long-ago day when a single sprig of sagebrush brought Nevada home to me, I have taken her no more for granted. Always when I return, one of the first things I must do is go out into the sagebrush until its chemistry works in me and I know I am home again. But now, older, I find myself reflecting whimsically on how very much like the sagebrush the people are, at least in the hinterland that makes up the most of Nevada, setting down roots and thriving in unlikely places, hardy and resilient, stubborn and independent, restrained by environment and yet able to grow free.

My daughter, whose turn it is now to go away and return,

tells me she is often an outcast in the society of students from settings of many people and little land.

"They are suspicious of us because we won't play their game of baring souls," she says. "Nevadans keep inside what's meant to be inside. We know who we are and where we came from, and they resent that. They would rather sit around and bounce their vibes off each other. They don't realize that they're suffocating because their emotions have nowhere to go. They don't know what it is to go out into the land and let your troubles fly away into the big silence."

I remembered a young cowboy I had met on a trip into the remote regions of northeastern Nevada. There, sixty miles from any paved highway, distance was measured by the time it took to travel by pickup truck or on horseback from one ranch to another, and a man was measured by his skill with a rope and how well he could stick out a bucking horse, and endurance.

I had watched the young cowboy that afternoon, running a stallion and mares and colts into a corral. The stallion had turned on him with snapping teeth and striking front hooves. He had evaded the attack, shaking out a loop with the dry comment, "This is one of them new-fangled nylon ropes. Seems to have some body. Not so bad at that." And then he had roped down that plunging mountain of bone and flesh as casually as if it were an everyday affair.

Yet, at supper that night, the young cowboy suddenly turned pale and could not eat. I followed him outside into the frozen night and asked him what was the matter. He answered in a voice tight with strain. "I've got to go away from here tomorrow. To the army. I've never been out there before."

What he did not say, but I understood, was that he was actually terrified. He was about to pay the penalty of being reared in a setting of isolation. My heart went out to him for what he would suffer, but after what I had witnessed that afternoon, I had no fears about the fact that he would survive. What he did not know—and I could not tell him—was that the land had already taught him the lesson of endurance.

2

The Explorers

IT was in these same forever reaches of northeastern Nevada that Hudson's Bay trapper Peter Skene Ogden, in 1826, may well have been the first white man to penetrate what is now Nevada. Some historians believe that he was. Others hold that trapper-explorer Jedediah Smith's crossing of the southern tip of Nevada in that same year marked the first entry by a white man. Some claim it was Francisco Garcés.

In any case, Peter Skene Ogden's trappers were not interested in exploration for exploration's sake. They were motivated more by search for beaver to satisfy the voracious appetite of Eastern fashion for gentlemen's beaver hats. Ironically, male plumage was the practical reason for expeditions into many of the West's hitherto uncharted regions. Ogden, a rough-hewn man with a quixotic nature that mixed brawling, drinking, and swearing with a penchant for quoting the Bible and Shakespeare to his men, is credited with discovering one of Nevada's main waterways in 1828. First known as Ogden's River, it was later renamed the Humboldt River in tribute to the famed German scientist by General John C. Frémont, an explorer and mapmaker with a compulsion for naming every landmark he encountered.

Unlike Ogden, Frémont's explorations in the decade from 1843 to 1853 probably had a secret national purpose, that of furthering the doctrine of Manifest Destiny, with its aim of taking everything—from Oregon to the Southwest—away from Mexico.

Frémont was the explorer who gave the name of Great Basin to the area that encompasses most of Nevada and parts of Utah, Oregon, Idaho, and California. He described it as a region of interior drainage in which rivers flowed inward to prehistoric lakes and sinks. In later times, geologists were to determine that the Great Basin had been formed a billion years ago by massive convulsions that thrust up at least a hundred nearly parallel mountain ranges, running from north to south and divided by great flatlands.

Frémont's mapmaking of the hostile environment of the Great Basin was to have implications more profound and far reaching than he could have dreamed. For the first time, a restless American populace east of the Missouri River, impoverished by the decimating depression of 1837, had actual maps to follow to the promised land that was California and the Pacific Northwest. Even the Mormon flight to Utah from religious persecution in Illinois was to be guided by Frémont's maps and descriptions.

The exodus from all points east did not begin with a bang. The first sizeable party to leave the jumping-off place in Missouri in 1841 numbered less than a hundred hesitant souls. But in the space of five years, the number of emigrants in a single party had mounted to three thousand. The rush to Oregon and California was on, never really to be stopped over the course of a century.

The first pioneers had not the slightest conception of the dangers and obstacles they would confront on the long journey westward. Some emigrant parties stumbled through with blind luck, finding forage and game and water in unlikely places. Others were not so fortunate, notably the Donner party.

In April of 1846, an emigrant train set out from Springfield, Illinois, bound for California. This wagon train, to be known in history as the Donner party, began its westward trek with only sixteen members. Along the trail it joined forces with other small wagon trains, until finally it numbered ninety men, women, and children.

Certainly the Donner party was lulled by the unexpected ease of the passage across the plains country. By the time it reached Fort Bridger in what is now Wyoming, impatience set in to reach California in the shortest time possible. The leaders of the party, two brothers named George and Jacob Donner, had been flirting along the way with a new book that had caused a sensation among prospective pioneers. It was entitled *The Emigrants Guide to Oregon and California*. Its author was one Lansford W. Hastings, who proposed a shortcut from Fort Bridger to Great Salt Lake, then across Nevada to California.

Hastings had indeed been a member of a wagon train which reached Oregon four years earlier. That much he acknowledged. What he did not acknowledge was that his return trip from California eastward across Nevada and Utah had been accomplished on horseback, without the encumbrances of a ponderous wagon train.

The Donner brothers chose to venture the shortcut despite warnings from knowledgeable mountain men at Fort Bridger. Their decision was to set in motion the grimmest mass tragedy of early pioneering. Instead of the seven days Hastings had said it would take to travel from Fort Bridger to Great Salt Lake, it took thirty days of exhausting toil through the rugged Wasatch Mountains. Instead of the one day Hastings had said it would take to cross the salt flats of Utah, it took six days of blazing heat and no water.

By the time the Donner party reached the meadows and springs near Pilot Peak on what is now the Nevada-Utah border, its members were near collapse. Precious days the pioneers lost in recuperating from this ordeal made for a delay compounded by their following another Hastings suggestion that cost a hundred needless miles in a circuitous route to the Humboldt River. By then it was the end of September.

With supplies nearly gone, the party sent two men ahead on what seemed an impossible mission—reach Sutter's Fort hundreds of miles away in California and return with provisions. Then, at Gravelly Ford on the Humboldt River, long-strained tempers flared, and a killing resulted. A man named James Reed, who had stabbed a team driver for striking Reed's wife, was banished into the desert without gun or food. It would have amounted to a sentence of death had not Reed's twelve-year-old daughter, Virginia, crept out at night to her father with a small sack of rations.

Harassed by Indians who ran off most of their cattle, the Donner party members somehow survived the long desert stretch between the Humboldt River and the Truckee River in western Nevada. When they reached the meadows where Reno now stands, their continuous string of bad luck was momentarily broken. One of the men whom they had sent to Sutter's Fort in California met them with food and mules. It was now late October.

Emaciated and exhausted, the Donner party members decided to rest before undertaking the last leg of the journey across the Sierra. It was their last and most fateful error.

The four days that would have taken them across the Sierra to safety in California were spent in the Truckee Meadows. When they roused themselves enough to begin the climb into the Sierra, the first snow of winter caught them. In panic they turned back to a mountain lake which in later times was to bear the name of the party, and hurriedly built rude shelters of brush and willows and wagon canvas. Then came a succession of storms that buried their hovels and suffocated their remaining animals in mountainous snowdrifts.

Two months passed before a party of seventeen men and women set out to climb the pass into California. In that intervening time, everything that was remotely edible was eaten— cattle frozen in the snow, wagon harness and leather shoes boiled to a pulp of little sustenance. The old and the very young died quickly, and were eaten by the survivors.

The escape party of seventeen fared no better. In the thirty-two days that it took to plunge through the drifts and cross the mountains, its members also turned to cannibalism. Only seven persons made it out of the snowline to a ranch on the Bear River in California.

The plight of the snowbound Donner party aroused a massive rescue effort from Sutter's Fort and among white settlers in northern California. Four relief parties made the trek across the snow-clogged Sierra hump to the lake, each bringing out survivors. One of the relief parties was led by James Reed, the man who had been banished from the wagon train. He had actually succeeded in crossing the Nevada deserts and the mountains into California. The rescuers wept at what they found at the lake—walking skeletons huddled in holes, and the ground littered with human bones. James Reed's daughter, Virginia, survived. Jacob Donner had died, and his brother George was too near death to be taken away by the rescue party. Despite the pleas of the rescuers, his wife chose to remain with him and die of starvation. It was now the end of February. The Donner party had been entombed in the Sierra snowdrifts for four months. Of the ninety members who had set out from Fort Bridger, six had died along the bitter route, and the Sierra had claimed forty-two more. When news of the Donner party's fate spread eastward, it was to deter pioneer travel for a long time to come.

Historians have long puzzled about the reasons why the Donner party did not reverse its direction and descend the mountains to the warm Nevada deserts. There, at least, the members could have found warmth and enough fish and game to keep them alive until spring. Perhaps the answer lies in the fact that in their minds, California meant civilization. The land they had passed through meant the unknown, and was therefore to be feared. It was an appalling penalty for pioneer ignorance.

Most early travelers to the west went to Oregon. Those bound for California followed the California Trail down to the Humboldt River that trapper Peter Skene Ogden had found, and from there, across Nevada to the Sierra range into California. Their lot was one of burning deserts, long stretches without water, little feed for animals, sparse game, and hostile Indians. But come they did, down the California Trail, scratching their names on rock walls as enduring memorials, and leaving a trail of unmarked graves and bleached bones of oxen as memorials of another sort.

In northeastern Nevada there is a rock wall that bears the names of these "westering" pioneers. They are mute, weathered reminders of another time and another people. Yet, in some unexplainable way, the presence of those names has cast its spell upon the land and the people who inhabit this lost corner of Nevada today.

In the important ways, the passage of time has made little impression upon the character of the people, many of them descendants of Mormon settlers who came after Frémont. To stay among them for a while is like stepping a hundred years into the past. One is caught with the fancy that the pioneers would have been right at home in this setting of far-flung ranches, houses made of logs and chinked with clay, stockade corrals and pole gates, leathery men with quizzical, judging eyes, women who get up in the darkness to cook huge breakfasts of sausage and eggs and homemade bread and pots of steaming coffee, and then go out to do a day's buckarooing in the saddle. Although church is an impossible distance away, they are deeply religious. They are gentle with their children, but restrictive in a way that would shock modern parents. Theirs is a way of talking that is not the diluted, obscure language of today, but old and pure and filled with imagery:

"I got me a good woman. She strung them fences with me like a man."

"He's a good boy, but, by Heaven, keep him down. Don't let him get no new ideas."

"Lordy, you're a sight for sore eyes. I'm glad you come a visitin'."

"Why, son, what do you want a fancy house for? Your Ma and me, we built our own, and it's been just fine all these years."

"So I says to this game warden, which breed I hate on principle, 'If you got a complaint, you tell it to me, not to that woman in there.' So he apologizes and a spell later, brings back a load of fish. So I says to him, 'I'll show you I got a heart as big as yours. You can stay for supper, and we'll cook 'em up.'"

"I do believe I got sawdust in my eyes. Time to go to bed."

3

The Old Heart of Nevada

T is in the hinterland that one finds the old heart of Nevada. Unlike Las Vegas and, to a lesser degree, Reno where the exodus from neighboring California and the westward movement of people have created cities of newly forming identities, migration to the hinterland has been slow.

Newcomers fleeing street crime, polluted air, and just plain too many people, enter with trepidation into places where generations of families with old values have left their stamp upon a small town. They encounter an attitude toward life that has changed but little over the span of a century. They meet Nevadans who are deeply protective of their birthright, suspicious of quick change, and who must judge a newcomer before they accept him, which takes time. It is a process that cannot be rushed.

Some leave, complaining of exclusion, but most remain and in time become indistinguishable from the longtimers. It is as though something in their makeup was Nevadan from the beginning.

The hinterland of Nevada is a country of far horizons broken only by mountain barriers lost in the haze of distance, and unexpected green valleys that break upon the traveler's eye with the breathstopping impact of a mirage. They are meandering belts of greenery where giant cottonwoods and quaking aspen and fragile willows line the banks of streams and rivers that are as

12

precious as gold in this land of little rain. Here, away from factories and pollution, the air is so clear that objects leap into view from miles away. A rock formation on a faraway rim of a hill becomes a pebble that one could reach out and pick up between his fingertips.

The small towns of Nevada, numbering from several thousand to a hundred inhabitants, are few and far between. A road sign on the outskirts bluntly proclaims:

NEXT GAS—91 MILES.

They are situated in the favored places where agriculture and mining still flourish, and where water is plentiful. They are quiet towns with white frame houses of the past on shaded back streets, interspersed with modern homes of the present. The pace of life is slow, and friends chancing to meet on Main Street have time to visit for a while before going on about their business.

The people who make up these towns are singularly what they are. The worst epithet that one can be branded with is that he is insincere. Virtues and faults are accepted as the human condition, and so are understood. But if one attempts to disguise them and present a pose of what he is not, then his company is shunned. Tellers of tall tales excepted. After all, liars' clubs were an institution of times before, and Mark Twain's legacy of exaggerated hoaxes in his newspapering days in Virginia City lives on.

Everyone must have his favorite small town, and Elko in northeastern Nevada is mine. In the near distance loom the turrets and minarets of the Ruby Mountains, green in summer, snow-buried in winter, and splashed in autumn with entire hillsides of golden aspen. At their base lies the hamlet of Lamoille, which in pioneer days was a detour trail when feed grew scarce along the Humboldt River. Here, buckaroos still drive their cattle down a doubtfully paved main street, and schoolchildren getting off the bus from school in Elko clump home in cowboy boots down the long lanes that lead to distant ranches.

Like so many Nevada towns, Elko came into existence in 1869

as a freighting and supply center for boom towns during the rich mining era of the 1860s. It was also home ground for such early-day cattle barons as John Sparks and Lewis ("Old Broadhorns") Bradley, both of whom became governors of Nevada. Bradley got his name from the herd of longhorn cattle that he trailed to Nevada in the 1860s.

The coming of the Central Pacific Railroad in 1868 cemented Elko's existence as a transcontinental stop. It also paved the way for exporting Nevada beef to San Francisco on the west and to lucrative eastern markets.

When the mining boom towns died away and agriculture began to replace mining as the mainstay of Nevada's economy, Elko slipped easily into its present-day role of a livestock capital, buttressed by a thousand square miles of cattle and sheep ranches.

Today it still retains its authentic frontier flavor of proper homes, banks and businesses, churches and schools, gambling casinos and saloons, and—no fooling—a red-light district of the old live-and-let-live tradition. A maze of livestock corrals lines the railroad track at one end of town, and shipping time is a furious time of dusty, shouting buckaroos and bawling steers, bleating lambs and the piercing whistles of Basque sheepherders.

This is beef and lamb country, where the steaks come big and tender and cooked out of long experience, and lamb is honest, tender lamb and not mutton. The standup bars in the saloons are lined at day's end with legitimate cowboys in scuffed, high-heeled boots and faded Levi's and the big hats that are coming back into style, and sheepherders with short-brimmed Stetsons and faces burned with sun and wind and cold. The mark of lonely existence is stamped on all their faces, and the conversations go:

"I got me a good price for them steers. That's the benefit of dealing with a buyer you like."

"You hear anything about old Wilson going belly up?"

"That's a durned shame. We used to run together in the old

*days, catching wild horses, stealing a few not so wild. We done
everything. Cowboyed a hell of a lot together.''*

*"This used to be open range. Now, them government bastards
has got everything parceled out. They wired a spring on the
Utah line I always used. It won't stay wired long, I promise
you.''*
*"Well, sometimes the law don't help, and a Winchester under
your leg is the only answer.''*

*"Them coyotes don't bother me. They don't eat grass. They eat
rabbits, and rabbits eat grass.''*

*"Sometimes, I think cowboys are all crazy. You know what that
wild sonofabitch of a Clel did? He piles into this ravine after a
steer at the same time little Dan is piling over the other side.
They met head on at the bottom, and horses and cowboys was
spread all over the map. I saw it happen, so I says to Clel afterwards, 'You could have avoided that run-in, and little Dan
wouldn't be hurt now.' And you know what he says to me?
'Well, I'm sorry about little Dan. But when I saw we was going
to have a head-on, I decided we might as well make it a good
one.' ''*

*"So Pete Itcaina, who was a big Basque sheepman in those
days, comes into this new saloon with his herders. They was all
dusty and sweaty from shipping lambs. The bartender, who
didn't like sheepherders, says he won't serve 'em, and he kicks
'em out. So Pete Itcaina goes straight to his lawyer and says,
'You know that new saloon down the street? I want you to buy
it.' The lawyer says, 'What do you want to do that for? You're a
livestock man.' Pete Itcaina says, 'You just call up the owner
and ask him how much he wants.' The lawyer does and tells
Pete Itcaina the price is $30,000, which was a small fortune in
those days, you know. Pete Itcaina says, 'You tell him we be
right over, and you make out a check, huh?' So they go over to
the saloon and give the check to the owner, and the owner signs
the deed over. Then Pete Itcaina goes out to the bar and says to*

the bartender, 'A little while ago, you were big boss man in this bar. You tell me to get out of here. Now, it's me who is big boss man, and I'm telling you to get out of my saloon.' Well, now, that's the most expensive drink that wasn't bought in Elko, but you got to remember Pete Itcaina didn't come to America to be treated like dirt.''

4

Cattlemen and the Pioneer Mould

ILL KNUDTSEN'S battered pickup had gone as far as it could go. There was no road. We were following the fenceline that ran up a low hill, down into a gully, and up another hillside. Our movement was slow and unhurried, tires rolling rhythmically over clumps of sagebrush and occasional rocks. As if keeping cadence with the motion of the pickup, Bill Knudtsen's talk was slow and unhurried, too.

When the pickup could climb no further in forward gear, Bill put it into reverse. The pickup backed down in a lazy sideways arc and went up the hill in reverse gear. The entire operation was so effortless that it did not even occasion a break in Bill's talking about the pioneers who had settled Grass Valley in central Nevada.

"They don't make 'em like those oldtimers anymore," he said. "Those people had to want to live here awful bad to go to all the work they did."

I wondered if the mould had really been broken, after all. His long frame in faded and torn Levi's and boots, his work-scarred hands, a stubble of beard on a face burned alternately by sun and cold, and a sweat-stained cowboy hat were testimony enough to the daylight-to-dark, seven-days-a-week routine that he kept. The settlers of this valley could not have worked very much harder in their struggle for existence.

We stopped to repair a break in the barbed-wire fence with a loop of baling wire, and Bill rambled along on his pet peeve, California deer hunters. "They shoot anything that flies or walks," he said. "With the open doe season, they've finished off nearly all the deer. There were even a dozen or so head of antelope up here, but they're sure as hell gone forever now. They will chop off the tops of fences to build a fire. Once, I cussed out a hunter for cutting through my fenceline to get inside to hunt. He said, 'Well, you don't have it posted.' And I said to him, 'Why, you sonofabitch. Do you put No Trespassing signs on your house to keep strangers from walking into your living room?' That shut him up. But anyway, I went ahead and put up No Hunting signs. And you know what they do? They take 'em home for souvenirs. Can you beat that?"

At the end of the fenceline, we took a detour down to a slender, winding meadow. At the end of the meadow, its back against a protecting hillside, was a pioneer house still standing. Its thick walls were made of stone, its roof was made of sod, and its adjoining corral of enduring cedar of varying lengths, lashed together to make a stockade. "With a little fixing," Bill said, "this house could be here another hundred years. When those pioneers made a house, they intended it to last."

We emerged to stand on the old wooden porch, and I noticed a road impossibly carved into the steep side of the mountain that flanked the meadow. "Oh, I got to tell you about that, because it's a real Nevada story," Bill said. "Seems that back then, there was a prospector who had his diggin's the other side of the hill behind this house. At first, he used to take the easy road through the meadow and this ranch to get to his diggin's. Then one day, the prospector had a falling out with the old man who owned the ranch, and the old man told the prospector he couldn't come through anymore. Well, you know what that prospector did? He took his pick and shovel and built himself that road on the side of the mountain. As the story goes, it took him a year to do it. And all the time he was working, the old man who owned this ranch would sit in his rocking chair, watching and chuckling while the prospector broke his back on that road. They never made peace. One just as stubborn as the other."

We descended to the valley floor, overlooking fields covered with great stacks of hay. Bill did not have to tell me the reason for that. No rancher from this part of Nevada to the northernmost extreme has not been told stories of the nightmare winter of 1889–1890 when blizzards swept the range with mountainous snowdrifts, to be followed by a freeze of 50 degrees below. Until then, ranchers had raised only token amounts of hay, depending upon winter forage in the deserts to tide their cattle and sheep through. But that year even the hardy range cows could not paw their way down to feed. I could remember a buckaroo called Old Button telling me, "It was a sight I never hope to see again. Them cattle came right down into the streets of Elko and Battle Mountain and Winnemucca, bawling out of starvation. And there was nothing to feed them. We shot them to put the poor things out of their misery. When the spring thaw came, the ranges was littered with thousands on thousands of carcasses of cattle and sheep. Everybody I knew went broke."

As we came into the main ranch, it was to see Bill Knudtsen's wife, Molly, coming home on horseback after a morning's buckarooing. Seeing Molly's seemingly delicate figure in tight-fitting chaps, boots, and spurs, it is hard to imagine that she performs the main buckarooing chores in all seasons on her Grass Valley ranch. It is harder to imagine that she is a former Eastern debutante who came to Nevada, was taken by the unadulterated nature and hard life of its backcountry people, and made her home here. In the tradition of Nevada backcountry women, she is a legend in a land where legends are hard to come by.

I have known other such women. One is Jesusa Saval, whose husband also ranged his stock in central Nevada. When her husband was killed, Jesusa Saval donned boots and spurs and ran the outfit with iron determination.

Another is elderly Rose Walter, who for many years was the last and only resident of the ghosted boom camp of Belmont in central Nevada. Rose Walter still lives alone in the thick-walled rock house where she was raised. The wooden planked floors are worn with the wear of a century, and the holes in them have been covered with tin cans flattened out and nailed down. A wood stove provides her with enough warmth to survive winters when the temperature dips to a minus 20 degrees.

Rose is the self-appointed law in Belmont, the guardian of tumbledown wooden shacks, a crumbling stone hotel, and a courthouse of better times. Tall and severe and unbent by age, she "runs the souvenir hunters off from these old places, because they belong to someone somewhere, you know."

Then there is Dr. Mary Fulstone, who came to Smith Valley in western Nevada in 1920. Few in this pioneer ranching valley and the country that surrounds it had ever heard of a woman doctor before she came, and fewer wanted to risk treatment at the hands of one. She got her start with Indians in their scattered colonies, having by tribal custom to consult with Indian medicine men before treating the sick.

But accidents and sickness and pregnancy will happen. Since that time of little acceptance, she has delivered more than four thousand babies, who represent a good share of the population of the ranching valleys. At the same time, she married and managed to raise a family of five children.

Despite her advanced years, she still practices medicine, making house calls over an immense area, treating patients at a new hospital in nearby Yerington or in the stately white frame house on her husband Fred's ranch. Dr. Mary, as she has come to be known, is a guest at the Indian housewarmings that are their graduation from the shacks in which they once lived. And today, many of the inhabitants of Smith Valley have never known what it is to be treated by any other than a woman doctor.

5

The Sheepmen

IT was one of those warm, golden days in the sagebrush desert of late summer, when the air was so bright that one's eyes had to draw into a squint to be able to support it. The desert was quiet and the silence broken only by the scraping of our boots on bare ground, and occasional talk. That was the trouble. Here, at least, it was too quiet.

I had known this sheep ranch since I was a boy. My father had trailed sheep through here on their way to summer range in the forested Sierra that reared in the distance. And more than once I had stopped here to rest and water the horses that I was driving from winter range to the foothills of the Sierra. Then, the ranch had always been a bustle of activity, corrals filled with milling sheep, the plaintive wails of lambs and the bleating of mothers looking for their wayward offspring.

Now, the ranch was deserted and the corrals abandoned. As we wandered through the maze of weathered brown boards and trampled earth, Batista said in his soft, outside voice, "I had to sell out. The Basque boys don't want to come over from the old country anymore, because life is getting better over there. They don't want to spend their best years out in the desert or the mountains herding sheep. You could say they were spoiled, but I can't blame them for not coming over. We didn't know it then, because there wasn't much choice for us, but I guess it was a hard life at that."

21

Out of long habit, he paused to straighten and close a gate to a corral that would never hold a head of sheep anymore and said with eyes narrowing in his creased face, "And then there was the coyotes. With that new law protecting them, they are all over the range. They was killing my lambs like rabbits, and there was no way we could stop them. You know yourself, one man with a rifle has no chance in hell to kill one of those things, much less a hundred of them. It was too discouraging, so I quit."

He was echoing a lament that can be heard throughout Nevada's range country today. Yet, it is only part of the reason for the decline of the sheep industry. The development of synthetic wools, uncertain world markets, importation of cheaper wool from foreign countries, and a lessening demand for mutton have all contributed to the decline. Dwindling from a peak of more than a million sheep in 1910, Nevada's sheep empires have vanished, and only a handful of outfits remain to tend less than two hundred thousand sheep on private land and on the diminishing public domain.

The story of sheep in Nevada was one that began almost by accident. The discovery that sheep could fare on the sagebrush deserts was made in the years of the California gold rush. Profits to be made by selling meat to the gold camps were realized by such as Kit Carson, who had been a scout for Frémont in his explorations of the Great Basin. In 1853, Kit Carson trailed some thirteen thousand sheep from New Mexico through Nevada to Sacramento, setting in motion a movement of half a million sheep across the Nevada deserts.

When the fortunes of the California gold camps waned and silver was discovered in 1859 near what was to become Virginia City, the sheep made a return journey over the Sierra to Nevada to feed the new boom camps. As mining strikes proliferated across the state's landscape, sheepmen followed. From then on, sheep were never again absent from Nevada.

The years immediately before and after the turn of the century were the years of biggest expansion in the sheep industry. They also saw the beginning of a period of violence between cattlemen and sheepmen over the scarce range forage and water of a desert state.

The range disputes were effectively settled in 1934 by the passage of the Taylor Grazing Act, which divided the open range between warring factions. From then on, cattlemen and sheepmen learned to live and prosper together. Contrary to the Hollywood-created myth of cowboy versus sheepherder forever, cattlemen often became sheepmen, sheepmen became cattlemen, and the most far-seeing ran cattle and sheep at the same time. It all depended upon the market, and both cattle and sheep used the same essentials of corrals and range and water. And sheep did not ruin a range, as the myth went. Instead, they were more delicate grazers than either cattle or horses.

I have known cowboys who herded sheep when buckarooing jobs were scarce, and sheepherders who became buckaroos when market prices for wool and mutton dropped and they in turn were left without jobs. My father and my uncles were typical. All of them came to America as young sheepherders. My father began with sheep, expanded to sheep and cattle together, and finally returned to sheep exclusively. Both of my uncles alternated between sheep and cattle until they died. All of them were good sheepherders and top buckaroos. And along the trail, they had all been riders enough to have tried their hand at the most demanding horseman's endeavor of all, running down and roping mustangs on the open range.

Though English, Scots, Irish, Mexican, and Chinese were predominant as herders in the beginning, the Basques emerged as the backbone of the range sheep industry. I once asked an English-born sheepman why this was so. He told me that of all the nationalities he had hired as sheepherders, he considered the Scots the most skillful. "But they and the Irish had a breaking point when it came to too much time spent alone," he said. "When they got fed up, they would walk away from their sheep and go to town for a tear. Not the Basques. They would stay with those sheep until they dropped in their tracks, or went nuts from being alone, or got rich. Usually, it was the latter."

The Basques have lived to see themselves regarded as a group unique to the Far West. But plagued by a lack of young herders and a public domain slowly being withdrawn for recreational uses, the tradition of the Basque sheepman on the open range will soon be a closed chapter in history. And the aspect of a sheepherder guarding his flocks through winter deserts and summer mountain meadows will have vanished forever from the Nevada scene.

"In them days, we no sooner got off the train from New York after the boat from the old country than we found ourselves out in the desert. We had our provisions, a bedroll, a carbine, strong walking shoes, an American hat, a burro, and a dog. And oh, yes, three thousand head of sheep. The boss would take a stick, and looking at that miserable desert stretching out there forever, he would scratch a map on the ground. To show where the water was, where the good feed was, and where the poisoned feed was. Then you just moved out. You got up with the stars so that the sheep could feed before the sun made the buds on the sagebrush and the little patches of grass too hot. That would change the taste, you know, and the sheep didn't like that. You took coffee then and came back in the middle of the morning and took bacon and eggs, which you had put in the burro's barley can so they wouldn't break. That was when the sheep was resting. Then they would get up and go again until nighttime. In a year we would walk thousands of miles. But that wasn't the hard part. The hard part was the loneliness. You would almost die from the loneliness, just to hear a human voice. Then a funny thing happened. You turned a corner in your mind, and you wouldn't walk over the next hill to see someone, even if they was someone there. They paid you thirty dollars a month and board. The room you didn't have to worry about. There was a lot of that around. Anyway, you made up your mind to suffer for that money, because you was poor. But poorer makes tougher, you know."

6

On the Mustang Trail

"*Back then, we used to turn our stallions out with the mustangs. You know, to build up the blood. In a couple years, we would get some damned fine saddlehorses out of them. But, Lord, they was tough to break with that wild mix in them. You would snub them down and twist their ear to make them stand still, then climb aboard and pray like hell. The best riders we had here was the Nigras and the Spanish boys, you know, Mexicans. There was one Nigra cowboy that was best of them all. He used to ride in the Fourth of July Rodeo in Reno. He would put a twenty-dollar gold piece between the sole of his boot and the stirrup. If he kept it there until he bucked the horse out, he would get to keep the money. That is one hell of a job of riding, I will tell you. But that's all he got to keep. They wouldn't let him compete for the prize money. The rule was against Nigras and Mexicans then, you know.*"

"*For a saddlehoss, the mustangs would durned near kill you on a long ride. They get you in the kidneys with their short walking. Shake you to pieces. But they was tough. They would go forever without getting tired, and they never sweat. Hoofs like iron. The mustangs did a big service for the cowboys, because they made the trails through the badlands, and them trails went straight. They didn't swing. They went the easiest and best way, but in a straight line, so the cowboys used them in those mean*

25

northern deserts to get to water. It was funny, but the mustangs would always go to water in the same place. They would put their front feet in, because they liked that mud water seeping up. But they kept their hind feet out, so that they could move in a hurry if they was mustangers about. You had to be careful when you roped them. Never get them in a hind leg, because they would pull the joint out. And fight! When them mustang stallions fought, they made a hell of a noise, screaming and stomping and sounding like they was eating each other up. They killed each other often, you know. Oh, the pretty colors on the wild ones in them days! You don't see many like that anymore. Now, they are all runted down and scrubby looking. Inbreeding and no feed, you know.''

"It was the first time I had been mustanging with Indians. They are some kind of riders, barrelling down off those rock slopes like the devil was after them. Well, this one day, they finally roped down this wild stallion they'd been after for a long time. They threw him down and tied him so he couldn't get up. Then they brewed up some coffee and sat around recreating the hunt, how smart that stallion was, how they had outfoxed him, and how double smart that stallion would be the next time around. When they were done talking, they upped and turned that stallion loose. You see, possessing the stallion wasn't what they were interested in. It was the chase, and that's all.''

"Before Congress made that Wild Horse and Burro law protecting them, I was a mustanger. My thinking was this: You've got to control the wild horse population. There's just not enough water and feed to support forty thousand head of wild horses in Nevada alone, mind you. When I was a mustanger, I kept the good ones and sold them for saddlehorses. And the old worn-out ones that I knew couldn't make the winter, I sold for dog-food. Like every other law they pass in Washington, it goes too far. You can't save all these mustangs. Winter is going to kill them like flies. You've got to cull them out.''

"You got to figure it this way. One mustang eats and drinks as much as one cow. With that new law protecting them, there are *jillions of mustangs around here. There is just not enough feed and water to take care of them and our cattle, too. The ranchers are up in arms, and you can't blame us. We got a right to make a living, too.''*

*T*ONY Amaral and I had left the capital of Carson City when the first rays of the sun were making a golden arc in the desert mountains to the east. Before the day was out, that jagged rim caught in outline was to be our destination. Leaving the paved highway, we took a winding dirt road through the sagebrush and up into the foothills, where the desert gray was broken by the stand of cottonwoods that was Black Hawk Springs.

There, one-time mustanger Wilbur Johnson was waiting for us with his wife, Marie, and young sons. The night before, they had trailered in the mustangs we were to ride in search of wild horses that are now mixed bloods of many strains, but still the descendants of the horse that Spanish conquistadores brought to America.

"If you are going to go after mustangs, then you had better use a mustang," Wilbur Johnson said. "Not only do they never give out in rough country, but for my money, a mustang caught is the best saddlehorse a man can have. A pasture horse will get uppity and throw you when you least expect it. But a mustang is loyal and predictable." He paused to quiet his own mouse-colored mustang stallion, who was nervous and snorting with impatience to be gone. "Hold still and try to act like a gentleman, which you ain't," he said, a white smile flashing in his deeply tanned face.

With the boys, Lance and Lorne, flanking out ahead, we took off across country. Still in their early teens, the boys in their big hats and spurs were like miniature cowboys. They were superb riders, and their task was to work the high mountain bluffs in the distance.

Moving at a short, choppy trot on a network of old mustang

trails cut deep into the rocky terrain, we mounted higher. The sky overhead was a vast dome of cloudless blue, and the sun was gentle with autumn. Once, a flight of chukar partridge roared up from a rim in front of us and winged down into a ravine like diving planes. Another time, four deer broke cover and bounded across our path with graceful dancers' leaps.

We saw our first mustangs at too great a distance. It was a band of mares of mixed coloring, roans and sorrels and whites and grays. Between them and us stood a black stallion with a white star on his forehead, his powerful neck arched and his attitude watchful and menacing.

Tony Amaral, who has spent years gathering stories of legendary mustangs and mustangers of Nevada's past, mused aloud. "He's a mean one. He reminds me of those stories about mustang stallions charging a man on horseback and almost biting his arms off."

But this stallion chose flight. Tossing his head with one last whistling snort of warning, he charged instead at his band of mares and herded them at a run into the almost impenetrable maze of rocks on the mountain rim.

We climbed toward that mountain rim, weaving up hillsides studded with huge boulders and slipping and sliding down slopes of shale rock in which our horses were buried fetlock deep. Tony Amaral, who had been a horse trainer for cowboy film epics, said dryly, "I don't know a stunt rider in Hollywood you could pay to come down slopes like this." And Wilbur Johnson retorted, "If those men in Washington who passed that antimustanging law had to take a trip like this or pile off one of these mountains at a dead run to put a rope on a wild hunk of horse, they would have some appreciation of a mustanger's life."

It was midafternoon before we finally got close to a mustang band, and then it was only because the wind was in our favor. We had come around a conical hill overlooking a desert hollow dotted with stunted pinion pine and clumps of juniper. A mile below us, almost hidden in the shade of a juniper with wide-spreading branches, were a stallion and a dozen mares and colts. Wilbur held up his hand in a signal, and we all dismounted quietly. The mustangs were dozing in the afternoon sun, and one colt was nursing at his mother's side. The stallion, a magnificent bay, seemed totally oblivious of our presence. The beaten earth around the tree revealed that it was a favorite resting place for mustangs.

We watched for a while, and then decided to see how near we could approach them before they spooked. Leaving our horses standing in the concealment of the conical hill, we crept down the slope by a circuitous route, keeping the wind in our faces. It was a punishing descent through brittle sagebrush and over rocks that clattered like plates at a wrong footfall.

When we reached the outcropping of rock that jutted out over the juniper tree, we inched our heads up to look down. The mustang band seemed almost at our feet.

It was a full minute before the stallion sensed that he was being watched. He lifted his nostrils to the wind, but could find nothing there. We crouched immobile, hardly daring to breathe. The stallion snorted uneasily, pawed the ground, and then made a searching circle around the perimeter of the juniper tree. Finding no sign of danger from the other directions, he returned to where he had started and stared in our direction. And then an incredible thing happened. The mares and colts came out of the shade to stand beside him with ears cocked forward, so that all of them were lined up facing us as if in a cavalry drill.

I will never know what finally spooked the stallion. Perhaps it was a chance shifting of the wind that brought our scent to him. Perhaps it was the instinct of the wild. Because suddenly, in a wild rush, the entire band stampeded up the side of the hollow and over the rim, leaving behind them a dusty vision of flying manes and tails, the harsh, dry clatter of unshod hooves, and the indelible memory of horses that had never known the binding of a rope or the confines of a corral.

In that one moment, it was as if I had had a backward glimpse into time and had seen the West as it once had been, in the free and untamed days of the first explorers.

7

The Fortune Seekers

$\mathcal{O}$FF the beaten track, at the end of those unmarked dirt roads that are forever branching off from the main highways, a hundred ghost towns dot the Nevada landscape. A collapsing hulk of a stone building, a scattering of brown-board shacks defeated by time and abandonment, the barely discernible remnant of a wide main street, a nearby hillside riddled with the black apertures of mine tunnels and littered with mounds of discarded rock, and the moaning of the desert wind in the encompassing silence are all that remain of the boom-and-bust towns that flourished and died in the wreckage of broken dreams.

An oddity of a sun-blackened prospector with a bristle of gray beard and the wisp of a hand-rolled rolled cigarette stuck in the corner of his mouth calls out from the wooden stoop of a shack, "Want to buy a town? I'll sell it to you for two bits."

How did this phenomenon come to be? That an actual town could vanish from the face of the earth more surely than if it had been bombed out of existence, because even bombed cities have a habit of growing back. But these did not, simply because their existence was as ephemeral as their reason for being in the first place.

One day a century and more ago, a prospector passed through in his interminable wandering and chipping at ledges and out-

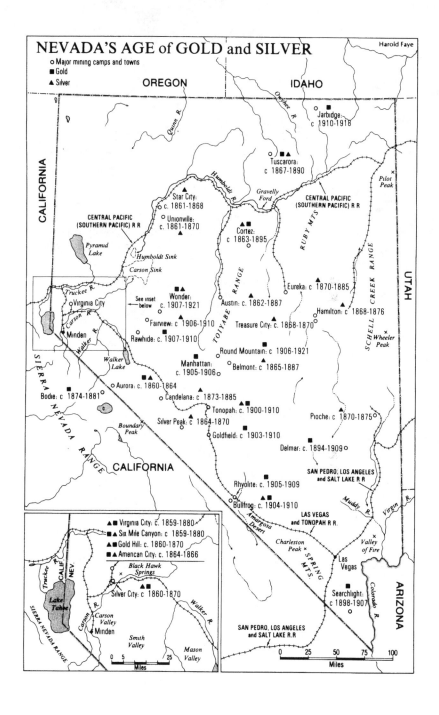

NEVADA'S AGE of GOLD and SILVER

Harold Faye

- o Major mining camps and towns
- ■ Gold
- ▲ Silver

OREGON   IDAHO

CALIFORNIA

UTAH

ARIZONA

Jarbidge:
c 1910-1918

Tuscarora:
c 1867-1890

Pilot
Peak ×

Quinn R.

Owyhee R.

Humboldt R.

Gravelly
Ford

CENTRAL PACIFIC
(SOUTHERN PACIFIC) R R

Star City:
c. 1861-1868

CENTRAL PACIFIC
(SOUTHERN PACIFIC) R R

Unionville:
c. 1861-1870

Cortez:
c 1863-1895

RUBY MTS

Pyramid
Lake

Humboldt Sink

Carson Sink

Eureka: c 1870-1885

Hamilton: c 1868-1876

SCHELL CREEK RANGE

Truckee R.

Virginia City

See inset
below →

Wonder:
c. 1907-1921

Austin: c. 1862-1887

Wheeler
Peak ×

Carson R.

Fairview: c 1906-1910

Treasure City: c. 1868-1870

Minden

Walker R.

Rawhide: c. 1907-1910

Round Mountain: c 1906-1921

TOIYABE RANGE

Manhattan:
c. 1905-1906

Belmont: c 1865-1887

Walker
Lake

SIERRA NEVADA RANGE

Aurora: c. 1860-1864

Bodie: c 1874-1881

Candelaria: c 1873-1885

Boundary
Peak

Tonopah: c. 1900-1910

Pioche: c 1870-1875

Silver Peak: c 1864-1870

Goldfield: c 1903-1910

Delmar: c. 1894-1909

CALIFORNIA

SAN PEDRO, LOS ANGELES
and SALT LAKE R R

Rhyolite: c. 1905-1909

Bullfrog: c. 1904-1910

Amargosa
Desert

LAS VEGAS
and TONOPAH R R.

Muddy R.

Virgin R.

Charleston
Peak ×

SPRING MTS

Valley
of Fire ×

Las
Vegas

Colorado R.

SAN PEDRO, LOS ANGELES
and SALT LAKE R.R.

Searchlight:
c 1898-1907

0   25   50   75   100
Miles

Inset (below)

▲■ Virginia City: c. 1859-1880
■▲ Six Mile Canyon: c 1859-1880
▲■ Gold Hill: c. 1860-1870
■▲ American City: c. 1864-1866

Black Hawk
Springs ×

Silver City: c 1860-1870

Truckee R.

CALIF.
NEV.

Lake
Tahoe

SIERRA NEVADA RANGE

Carson R.

Carson
Valley

Minden

Walker R.

Smith
Valley

Mason
Valley

0   5   25
Miles

croppings of rock. The prospector had probably been a latecomer to Virginia City's Comstock lode in the 1860s, arriving at a time when all the silver-bearing land in sight had already been claimed. So, like hundreds of others, he had set out into the deserts in search of another Virginia City.

If a chip looked promising in silver—but he could not be sure because he was not well enough equipped to know—it went into the packbags on his burro with a mental note of where he had found it in the vague terrain of confusing sameness.

When the prospector got to a town, his first order of business was the visit to the inevitable assay office, that dispassionate maker or breaker of dreams. If the assay test was negative or halfhearted, the chips of rock went out the window. But if one among them was really promising, it was a glimmer of hope that set the prospector racking his brain to remember exactly where he had found that one rock out of a hundred.

If he could remember, it was usually enough to get a grubstake, because a prospector was broke much or all of the time. He would never dream of entering the portals of a bank. That was a world to which his station denied him entrance. So, it was usually a saloonkeeper or a gambler whose way of life was one of betting on the come.

When he got his grubstake, the prospector went back into the desert, newly provisioned and leading three burros this time. If his memory had not betrayed him, he found the ledge and followed it along to determine if his promising chip was a splash of color or an honest-to-goodness vein. If it were a vein, it would at one point disappear into the earth, and so he tunneled down as far as safety would allow before a cave-in could trap him. Then he staked his claim, scribbling out an almost illiterate message on a scrap of paper, putting it into a tobacco can and burying it under a cairn of rocks. Then the long trek back to town and the confirming visit to the assay office.

If the test proved out rich, the prospector's elation was mingled with fear. Most times, the assayer could be counted upon to keep the secret. But if there was doubt, then a sure way of buying silence was to cut the assayer in for a share of what was to come. The prospector could have bypassed his grubstaker, but that was pretty fair insurance of a bullet in the back somewhere down the line. And anyway, to find silver was one thing. To get it out of the ground was something else that added up to working capital. So back to the grubstaker.

Now, the need for secrecy against the revealing mechanics of getting ready to work the mine properly: the filing of the claim, the grubstaker's drawing out or borrowing of a substantial amount of money from the bank, buying of mules, wagons, picks and shovels, dynamite, provisions, lumber to shore up the tunnels, and, most risky of all, the hiring of experienced miners to do the hard work.

If the prospector and his grubstaker were lucky, they managed to sneak out of town at night without being followed. This was no easy feat, because there were many weak links in the chain and the antennae of men in mining country are sharply attuned to any unusual activity.

When the remote ledge was reached by the prospector and his partner, the immediate priority was the staking out of as many surrounding claims as the law allowed. Then, the necessity of protecting these claims from claim-jumpers, usually over the sights of a rifle. After that dispute was settled, the prospector and his partner couldn't care less who found out. Now that they were secure, they needed many people for many reasons. And the rush was on.

First came the fortune-seekers, miners trained and untrained, staking their claims in the gullies and along the hillsides, putting up tents or digging sagebrush-covered hovels in which to sleep and cook. After them came the merchants and the first freight wagons, bringing in meat and fresh vegetables and flour, mining tools and more lumber for the tunnels and deepening shafts. Lumber, too, for the builders who threw up one-room shacks, flophouses where a man could buy a few hours sleep in a real bed before surrendering it to the next man, bathhouses with hot water in wooden tubs in preparation for the Saturday-night whingding. Because by this time, the saloonkeepers, the gamblers, and the prostitutes had determined the place was worth coming to. They were not unwelcome. In a community of men, their services were indispensable.

If the strike bore out, there was a point at which the crude knowhow of the first miners would reach its limit. No surface placer mining here on streams and rivers, like in the California goldfields, because Nevada silver had a habit of going deep underground. There was a need for trained engineers who could shore up a shaft and tunnels with the new square-set timbering that Virginia City had developed, metallurgists who knew how to go about the job of extracting silver from companion minerals, and men who could cope with the building of such a technical thing as a mill. Their price did not come cheap, so the prospector's share, probably diluted several times by now, was diluted again.

The arrival of educated professional men—engineers, metallurgists, doctors, lawyers, and the ubiquitous mining-camp newspaperman with a handpress and a "shirttail full of type"— marked the day of schism in the new town. They built their homes in a section apart from the miners' shacks, saloons, and prostitutes' cribs. When their homes were built, they sent for their wives and children, and that in turn meant schools and a church or two.

It was only when the signs of permanency were fairly certain that the California bank crowd moved in with big money and big plans, which usually amounted to buying up claims by the dozen or making loans for equipment in exchange for shares in a profitable mine. At this point, the prospector and his partners had to make a choice of selling out for a small fortune or making a new partner whose investment money might double that fortune for all concerned. Because riches of the sudden variety usually breed the desire for even more riches, they chose the latter course.

When the big money made its appearance, so did that bane of all mining camps, the speculator of mining stocks. Some were honest, but most used every trick in the swindler's book to milk savings from the little people—stock juggling, rumors and sucker articles in the local newspaper about a fabulous new strike, selling and buying on the San Francisco stock market, so that nobody except them ever knew for certain what was the truth and what was a lie. But one thing was certain. In the end, the stock speculator would make more money than anybody else in town, without ever once having to muddy his hands in the earth.

When the town reached its zenith, it was like Virginia City all over again. The pervading atmosphere was that of a carnival that would never end. The bankers, professional men, wealthy merchants, and the new-rich prospectors and their backers kept to their own with fancy-dress balls, lobster and caviar brought all the way from San Francisco, and even imported French champagne. But the other side of the tracks degenerated into a bedlam of ceaseless carousing and knife- and gunfights.

Somewhere along the line, the law had made its appearance, but it was usually an unobtrusive one. By now, there was that kind of man in town who was more adept at the business of killing than a sheriff or a marshal. When the shootings and the knifings got out of hand, it became time for respectable men to form a vigilance committee. In a week or a month, the committed solved the problem of lawlessness by the simple expediency of hanging a few men under cover of night and pinning a paper saying *601* on their chests. That ominous number, borrowed from a California vigilante group of 601 members, was usually warning enough to any potential troublemaker to mind his manners or leave town in a hurry.

Then would come the day of the disturbing rumor that the unending treasure in the earth was beginning to play out. Some were sobered, but most people refused to believe the carnival could ever end. The bankers and the speculators were the first to know, and their departure gave substance to the rumor. After them, almost guiltily, went the engineers, the lawyers, the newspapermen, and the doctors. Then one morning, the town would wake up to find that half a dozen stores had been closed in the night. That, finally, was the spark that touched off the exodus.

Because they were mostly immigrants who could not adapt that quickly to change—Germans, Irish, Cornishmen, French, Spanish, and Italian—the working miners were among the last to realize that the town was done. When they went, so did the purveyors of booze and flesh and excitement. The last to leave were the Chinese who had never caught the contagion of sudden wealth, but who did have patience. They remained only long enough to pick over the great mounds of tailings for the last bits of silver that might remain. Even the Indians who had worked at menial labor preceded them, trailing back into the desert from which they had come.

Later, the big houses that had once been occupied by the wealthy were bought and moved one by one to more permanent towns that did not rely on the elusive stuff of silver and gold for their existence. Other houses were stripped brick by brick and carted away by scavengers. Finally, all that was left was what could not be moved, like a stone courthouse, or was not worth moving, like the miners' shacks. Time and the desert wind will do for them.

Out of the myriad Nevada boom towns that were born in the frenzied 1860s and 1870s, or later when history repeated itself in the Tonopah-Goldfield strikes of 1900, only a few have managed to survive. Logically, the first and biggest of them all, Virginia City, should have been the first to die. Instead, it has managed to cling to life, sometimes precariously, to the present day. The age of tourism came along in time to serve as its salvation.

Virginia City is where Nevada really began. Until the discovery in 1859 of silver near where Virginia City now stands, Nevada was simply a place to be gotten through as quickly as possible on the way to golden California. Its only inhabitants were native Indians and the several thousand farmers, ranchers, trading-station keepers along the pioneer trails, and a small band of disillusioned miners who had washed back from California.

In the decade that went before, there had been rumors of gold in the desert canyons of western Nevada. Nothing of substance was found, and the miners who came to explore the canyons were few and haphazard in their efforts. There seemed to be promise in what was whimsically known as Gold Canyon, but the sparse gold was mixed with a heavy black mud that discouraged the labors of the miners. The mud was thrown aside in disgust. It was only by chance that when the winter snows came and the miners returned to California, someone went to the trouble of taking a few handfuls of the mud along for assaying. The tests did not show much gold, but they revealed something else. The "mud" was incredibly rich in silver.

Until that day, all the wagon roads had led to California. Now, they changed directions and converged upon Gold Canyon in Nevada. Early chronicler J. Ross Browne, in his writings *A Peep at Washoe and Washoe Revisited,* described the rush to Washoe, as western Nevada was then known:

> An almost continuous string of Washoeites stretched like a great snake dragging its slow length as far as the eye could see. Parties of every description and color were noted: Irishmen wheeling their worldly goods on wheelbarrows: Americans, Frenchmen, and Germans on foot leading horses heavily packed; Mexicans driving long trains of pack mules; dapper-looking gentlemen riding fancy horses; women dressed in men's clothes mounted on mules or burros; organ grinders; drovers; cripples and humpbacks; and even sick men got up from their beds all stark mad for silver.

And they found it. In the twenty years that followed, nearly $300 million in silver and gold was taken from the rocky, sagebrush-covered mountains that surround Virginia City. In the process, a fantastic town of stately mansions, luxurious hotels, gourmet restaurants, schools, churches, stores, an opera house, roaring mills, and sophisticated mine operations rose out of non-descript shanties in the shadow of Sun Mountain.

It was here that the stage celebrities of yesteryear—Sarah Bernhardt, Lillian Russell, Lotta Crabtree, and John Wilkes Booth's brother Junius—trod sloping stages to entertain newly made millionaires in red-velvet boxes and crudely garbed miners crowded into the cheap seats. And it was here, as a Virginia City newspaperman, that Mark Twain got his start, rising from an obscure reporter with a penchant for writing satirical hoax stories and lampoons of famous figures.

This was the town and this was the wealth that were to transform Nevada from a neglected part of Utah Territory to territorial status of its own, precipitate early statehood in 1864, a mere

five years after the discovery of silver, and enrich an impoverished Union treasury in the Civil War.

Out of the Comstock's furious activity were born many in-
novations that were to affect the world of mining. Digging in
deep shafts had always been hazardous because of the threat of
cave-ins, and the Comstock was no exception. When miners
passed the one-hundred-foot level, they lived in constant fear
that the soft earth in which they dug would collapse and bury
them alive.

A German engineer named Philipp Deidesheimer was summoned from California to devise a new method for deep mining.
He arrived at an ingenious principle of constructing open-sided
squares braced by heavy timbers. When one square was set into
the ground, another could be connected to it. This enabled the
miners to move downwards or sidewards in safety while following the devious course of a vein. The process was not unlike
that of children's building blocks going down instead of up.

The Comstock also saw huge forward leaps in the technique
of extracting silver and gold from raw ore. The crude method of
crushing ore by mortar and pestle and boiling it together with
extracting ingredients such as quicksilver and copper sulphate in
a large kettle was refined and enlarged upon. Mills capable of
crushing huge amounts of ore and extracting precious metals
with the aid of steam proliferated to the point where nearly a
hundred such operations surrounded Virginia City.

Compressed-air drills developed on the Comstock had a two-
fold benefit. Not only were they more efficient in the task of
digging out ore, but they helped to ventilate the deep shafts with
air from the surface. Before, miners could only work fifteen
minutes at a time in a situation of intense heat and lack of fresh
air; and to compensate for the resulting dehydration, the miners
consumed in a single day a prodigious amount of ice water.

One of the first successful western mining labor unions also
saw its appearance in the era of the Comstock. Until then,
organized labor movements in western mining camps had been
marked by failure, mainly because of their inability to recruit
members. The formation of the Virginia City Miner's Union
was more organized, and the union proved to be strong enough

to bargain for better wages and working conditions. The union's success was to start a trend that would have a far-reaching impact on western mining

And then, late in 1877, the decline began. The veins of the Comstock lode and the Big Bonanza ore body—one of the richest in recorded history—started to pinch out, silver prices skidded, the mines and mills fell silent, and the exodus came. By 1900, Virginia City, the Queen of the Comstock, was a shabby dowager stripped of her elegance and reduced from ten thousand courtiers to a few hundred faithful who refused to give up obeisance to the glory of what once had been.

It is a cynical commentary that out of the billion and more dollars taken from the Nevada earth in its boom days, little of it was sown back. The exception was the family of John Mackay, an Irish immigrant who started as a lowly miner and by dint of hard work and shrewd investments, became one of the Bonanza kings of the Comstock. After Mackay's death in later years, his widow and son became the first major benefactors to the University of Nevada. They founded the Mackay School of Mines and gave funds for a science building and an athletic stadium. In this, they were following in John Mackay's tradition of generous giving to community projects and hundreds of down-and-outers during his years on the Comstock.

When the Comstock busted, a score of millionaires took their new-found money and departed to gentler climes, leaving behind them a plundered land and a floundering state fighting through a long depression to preserve even the semblance of statehood.

8

A State Is Born

"Oh, the Mormon roses and the Mormon poplars! Wherever the Mormons went, they planted. Wherever they have been, there roses bloom."

*T*HE Mormon poplars still stand, and the roses still bloom in the green valley that presses against the snowtipped peaks of the Sierra. Here it was that Mormon colonists established the first permanent settlement in what was to become Nevada, calling it Mormon Station and later changing its name to Genoa.

Not three years after the signing of the Treaty of Guadalupe Hidalgo by which Mexico, in 1848, ceded the western lands to the United States, the Mormons had been sent out from Salt Lake City on their colonizing mission. They went dutifully into the wilderness that marked the extreme western extension of Utah Territory, erecting a fort for protection against Indians, clearing and planting the fertile valley lands, and establishing a trading post to sell fresh produce and meat to the wagon trains bound for California.

In the several years that followed, the Mormons extended their domain along the valley chain that lay under the shoulder of the Sierra, even building a sawmill at another settlement

40

called Franktown to provide lumber for houses and farm build-ings. Life in the colonies was marked by hard but rewarding work. The colonies were models of efficiency and shared goals, with an underpinning of stern administration and meting out of punishment to breakers of the common code. The colonies flourished so well that Mormon leaders in Salt Lake City met in convention to organize a territorial government and create what they called the State of Deseret for governance of the western Mormon colonies.

Brigham Young, church leader and governor of Utah Terri-tory, even sent one of his Twelve Apostles, Orson Hyde, to preside over what he had designated, in 1854, as Carson County Court. Despite the appearance of non-Mormon gentiles who had washed back from the California gold rush, it seemed that Mor-mon control was firmly fixed in western Nevada.

More gentiles came, settlers who had remarked upon the fer-tile valleys in their passage through to California and fortune seekers in search of gold. Friction between Mormons and gentiles was inevitable. The latter bridled under what they termed the tyranny of Mormon rule. Mormon allegiance naturally turned toward Salt Lake City, and in retaliation, there were rumblings among the gentiles favoring annexation to neighboring Califor-nia. Politics began to mix with the pastoral in the peaceful set-ting.

Then, in 1857, an event occurred that was to launch one of the most bizarre and crazy-quilt patterns ever to mark the beginnings of a state. In that year the growing tensions between Governor Brigham Young in Salt Lake City and the federal gov-ernment in Washington, D.C., suddenly threatened to erupt into armed warfare. The confrontation between Brigham Young and President James Buchanan had been inevitable. Since the time the Mormons had settled Utah, their leader had resented federal jurisdiction over what he considered Mormon domain. Much of the dispute proved later to be clouded by misunderstanding, but for the time being, both Buchanan and Brigham Young pre-ferred to take obstinate stands. Young promptly dispatched mes-sengers on fleet horses to call the Mormon faithful home to defend Salt Lake City against six thousand federal troops approaching over the Oregon Trail with orders to enforce federal law in Utah Territory.

The hold of the Mormon Church over its adherents was so strong that only a few resisted the summons. In western Nevada, the Mormon departure was almost total. Some men actually came in from their fields, paused long enough to load up wagons with family and a few possessions, and raced headlong to Salt Lake City. Their farms were left abandoned. Other Mormons, sensing that there would be no return, lingered to sell their hard-won lands and homes to the gentiles for next to nothing. Still others, dreaming of return, arranged what they mistakenly thought would be binding leases for their properties.

As it turned out, the Mormon departure was not even necessary. The threatened punishment of Brigham Young was never carried out. Not a shot was fired in the heralded war between the Mormons and the federal government. Misunderstandings were cleared up, and negotiations ended in a truce. The troops were dispersed to the Presidio in San Francisco and to Arizona.

In western Nevada, Mormon control vanished in the wink of an eye. No sooner had the Mormons left than the growing number of gentiles met in Genoa, in 1857, to adopt a constitution for a new Territory of Nevada, to be carved, naturally, out of their parent Territory of Utah. The attempt at separate territorial status was unsuccessful, but it accomplished something else. The gentiles had at least become a cohesive entity bent upon self-government.

When a number of the original Mormon settlers returned to western Nevada a year later, they found themselves not only stripped of their lands but also of their authority. To add to their woes, the discovery of silver near Virginia City had touched off the silver rush to Nevada. The vastly outnumbered Mormons gave up all hope of reclaiming any vestige of their pioneering colonies. Even their legacy of ordered community life and honest courts was gone. Violence and thievery and murder went virtually unpunished, and whatever remained of judicial procedure was a farce. Corruption became the order of the day, and few were the jury verdicts that had not been purchased in hard coin. The disintegration of all that they had striven to build was the final blow for the returning Mormons. Only a handful chose to remain. The rest trailed back to Salt Lake City or made their way to Mormon communities where order and justice still prevailed.

In the summer of 1861, a select entourage of people converged by different routes upon the newly created Territory of Nevada. Though they came from varied locales, they shared a common goal—that of preparing a territory for statehood.

The silver rush had prompted the Congress to move quickly in passing legislation creating the Territory of Nevada. President James Buchanan signed the bill on March 2, 1861, as one of his last acts in office. The fact that the population of the new territory numbered but 20,000 souls—one-sixth of the requirement for even a single representative in Congress for the state-to-be— was of minor concern. The fact that the territory's rich mines were producing millions of dollars a year in silver and gold was somewhat more important.

There was also the factor of a small but outspoken coterie of secessionist sympathizers in an unorganized territory ripe for the picking. Something had to be done quickly to head off the secessionists and enlist Nevada in the Union cause. The newly elected president, Abraham Lincoln, was prepared to do just that. One of his first acts on taking office in 1861 was to appoint a territorial governor for Nevada, James W. Nye.

Nye headed the larger segment of the Nevada-bound entourage. They traveled in comparative luxury, by ship from New York City, overland across the Isthmus of Panama, and by steamer to San Francisco. The bulk of Nye's official family, which numbered about a dozen officeholders and their aides, had been recruited from no less than seven states by a curious set of circumstances.

In the contest for Republican candidate for president, Nye had actually worked for Lincoln's opponent, William Seward, the U.S. senator from New York. Despite Seward's reputation and Nye's vaunted skill as a campaign manager, Lincoln won the nomination. Nye then worked fervently for Lincoln's election, became his close friend and confidant, was commissioned a brigadier-general, and from then on was on an affectionate "General" and "Abe" relationship with Lincoln.

It was typical of Lincoln that he appointed his former opponent, Seward, to the post of secretary of state. Seward paid off his political debt to James Nye by obtaining his appointment as governor of the Territory of Nevada. Nye, in turn, paid off his own political due bills by naming campaign workers from various states to his official family, with one exception.

That exception was a man named Orion Clemens, a lawyer and one-time newspaper publisher in Missouri. Clemens had stumped Missouri in support of Lincoln. As reward, Lincoln's newly appointed attorney general, Edward Bates, obtained the appointment of Orion Clemens as secretary of state of the Territory of Nevada.

Orion Clemens did not travel with the Nye party. By steamboat and stagecoach, he made his way overland to Nevada in the company of his brother Samuel, a sometime newspaperman and river pilot who had agreed to serve as Orion's private secretary. In his obscure post, Samuel Clemens could not have dreamed that the Nevada experience would one day propel him into worldwide fame as a writer named Mark Twain.

As Samuel Clemens was later to record, he and Orion were limited on their overland journey to twenty-five pounds of baggage each, which consisted mainly of the clothes on their backs, Orion's Colt revolver, Samuel's Smith and Wesson seven-shooter, blankets, pipes and tobacco, a shot bag of silver coins, some U.S. statutes, and an outdated Webster's Abridged Dictionary "weighing one thousand pounds."

Governor James Nye and his party were not quite so limited. As befitted their official role, they had set out with so much baggage and paraphernalia that they were forced to wait in San Francisco for another ship to arrive with the residue, including the official papers for organizing the territory.

The dalliance in San Francisco did not turn out to be unwelcome. Nye's party was made up mostly of unattached young men. They were lionized and feted by the city's politicians and society set. Nye reciprocated in kind with the good-humored Irish oratory for which he was famous. His personal appearance worked as an asset, too. Samuel Clemens, in *Mark Twain's Autobiography,* described him:

> He was a striking-looking man with long white hair, a friendly face, and deep, lustrous dark eyes that could talk a native language, the tongue of every feeling, every passion, every emotion. His eyes could out-talk his tongue, and this is saying a good deal, for he was a very remarkable talker, both in private and on the stump. He was a shrewd man.

Shrewd as he was, Nye was to encounter in his San Francisco stay one man who was shrewder. His name was William Stewart, a Nevada attorney domiciled in a town called Carson City.

Unknown to Nye, William Stewart was something of a local legend in the territory. Yale-schooled, he had come west with the California gold rush and then to Nevada in the silver rush. He was a man of powerful physical stature, standing six feet, two inches and weighing two hundred pounds. Red-bearded and hot-tempered, he had earned a reputation in the gold camps as a rough-and-tumble fighter. His fearlessness had been amply demonstrated in an incident that occurred while he was helping to prosecute an accused murderer on trial in the Genoa court.

One of the accused's closest friends was a notorious killer named Sam Brown, reputed to have killed thirteen men in Texas and California before coming to Nevada. Boasting that he would free his friend at the point of a gun, Sam Brown rode from Virginia City to Genoa and swaggered into the courtroom. Such was his reputation that jurors and spectators alike dived under benches or out of the window.

Stewart did not join them. Standing with his arms crossed in front of the judge's bench, he waited while Sam Brown approached. Then he unfolded his arms to reveal that most lethal of close-range weapons, a derringer, in each hand. Brown was escorted to the witness stand. His testimony, elicited by Stewart's questioning, helped to convict the accused murderer. When it was over, Stewart escorted Sam Brown back to the door at gunpoint and sent him on his demoralized way. As chance would have it, Sam Brown took a sulking shot at an innkeeper on the ride back to Virginia City. The innkeeper, one Henry

Van Sickle, retaliated by blowing Sam Brown apart with a shotgun, thereby earning the praise of a local coroner's jury.

Because none of his official family was from Nevada, Nye had no inkling of the fierce tug-of-war as to where the capital should be located. William Stewart took quick advantage of Nye's delayed arrival in Nevada Territory. He journeyed quietly to San Francisco to meet the new governor. With the brilliant persuasive power that was later to make him a titan in the U.S. Senate, Stewart convinced Governor Nye that the territorial capital should be located at Carson City instead of the logical site, Virginia City. As a clincher, Stewart invited Nye to be his houseguest in Carson City until he was settled. Convinced and charmed, Nye accepted the invitation, thereby giving Carson City a psychological edge in the argument over the permanent location of the capital when the territory became a state. Carson City already had something of an advantage in that the Utah legislature had designated it as the county seat for the western extension of Utah Territory.

Governor Nye's enthusiasm was more than a little dampened when he finally got to his temporary capital. Conceived only a short time before, Carson City was a small collection of white frame buildings, a few brick ones, an unfenced town square with a liberty pole in its center, and a remarkable number of mythical, untenanted streets. However, the residents gave him a warm welcome replete with an open-air champagne reception at Genoa, booming cannon, and a procession to Carson City for his official family. After a short stay with Stewart, as promised, they installed him hastily in Nevada's first governor's mansion, a one-story, two-room, white frame house.

If Nye regretted his decision, he nevertheless stuck by his word, even when the Queen of the Comstock, Virginia City, tried by every device to change his mind. Nye's welcome in Virginia City was the most elaborate event the town had ever staged. There was a procession that included a brass band, the Union Guards, and a floral arch, no less. Afterwards there was an elaborate banquet in which champagne flowed like water.

Virginia City's politicians and foremost residents may have hoped to get Nye drunk enough on this and future occasions to relocate the territorial capital in Virginia City. They were doomed to failure. After one bout, which found Virginia City's elite under the table and Nye still on his feet, he remarked, "They don't know me. I am familiar with champagne and have no prejudices against it."

Though Nye had the right to designate the territorial capital, the issue of where the state capital should be located was settled by a territorial council. It chose Carson City. Again, Stewart's hand was probably at play in the final designation. Historians have speculated that he was instrumental in promising county-seat status to a number of towns in exchange for their delegate's vote to make Carson City the permanent capital.

Being by nature a long-suffering man, Orion Clemens upon his arrival was not disconcerted by the rough frontier aspect of Carson City. In the same room where he slept, he set up the office of secretary of state, serving without pay until a legislature could be convened to appropriate money for salaries. Orion later reminisced that whenever the wind blew, a sheet of paper in his joint office-bedroom was soon covered with dust. And in the winter, the snow blew in through the window sills and settled on the roof, and then melted and dripped down on his papers. He said the stove smoked so much that after making a fire in the morning, he could not see for a while from one end of the office to the other.

Governor Nye and the rest of his official family were in the same financial straits as Orion Clemens. Their meager personal savings were soon gone. From then on, all of them ate "on the cuff" at a local boardinghouse. This state of affairs, coupled with public jokes about political carpetbaggers, did not do much for their dignity. Even before the legislature had convened, most members of Nye's entourage had wandered away. Some went to Virginia City to try their hand at mining, and the remainder either went home or back to the good life in San Francisco. Soon, all that were left were Governor Nye and Orion Clemens, the latter serving simultaneously as secretary of state, treasurer, comptroller, and acting governor. The last role was thrust upon Clemens by Governor Nye's frequent visits to San Francisco on so-called matters of state. Also, the long Nevada winters so aggravated his arthritis that he was compelled to seek relief in warmer climates. It was not a very auspicious beginning for government in Nevada.

When the territorial legislature finally met in October of 1861, the situation was not markedly better. It met in a barnlike structure with sawdust on the floor, which took the place of spittoons that could not yet be afforded. The meeting room was heated by stoves borrowed from the territorial government in Utah. The two houses of the legislature—territorial council and house of representatives—were divided by canvas partitions. The legislative body was so impoverished that the first major dispute concerned the paying of $1.50 a day to a clergyman for saying the opening prayer. The clergyman was, in fact, dismissed when the legislature learned that one of its members was an Episcopal minister who would pray for free.

Still and all, the legislature accomplished most of what it set out to do, in spite of Mark Twain's later description that it "levied taxes to the amount of thirty or forty thousand dollars and ordered expenditures to the extent of about a million." It divided the territory into nine counties, established county seats, listened patiently to Governor Nye's plea that establishing a system of common schools and teachers would be cheaper than establishing prisons and paying keepers, and then promptly established a prison. Somewhere in the process, however, the most important duty was performed. The necessary legislation was passed to organize the new Territory of Nevada.

In the intervening three years between territory and statehood, Nevada assumed a role of crucial importance in the national eye. With the outbreak of the Civil War, both the Union and the Confederacy were engaged in a desperate power play to draw the western lands into their respective folds. Because of its new-found mining wealth, Nevada was key in that power play. But there was something equally as important at stake from President Lincoln's political point of view. He needed Nevada's votes as a full-fledged state to help him uphold the Emancipation Proclamation of 1863. Sentiment in the Congress for a Constitutional amendment abolishing slavery was dominant. However, a two-thirds vote in both houses was needed, and votes from Nevada's three-man delegation in Congress could swing the decision. Lincoln quickly pushed through an enabling act to make Nevada a state. All that was required to finalize the action would be the drafting of a constitution acceptable to the citizenry of the territory.

A popular poll had revealed that Nevada's sentiment was pro-Union. However, the situation still remained volatile in the territory. Clashes between Union supporters and secessionists were frequent. Only a few years before, secessionist recruits had even attempted to take over Virginia City by arming three buildings as forts. The attempt had failed mostly from lack of citizen support, but strong feelings remained on either side of the issue.

Nevada's first constitutional convention, assembled hurriedly, met in late 1863. Its makeup was typical of mining-rush country. The delegates included eight lawyers, four miners, five merchants, two farmers, one hotel keeper, one physician, one notary public, one coach maker, one engineer, one lumberman, and one sign painter. All were recent arrivals in the silver rush to the Comstock lode.

Although Lincoln faced a national crisis in the battle over his antislavery amendment to the U.S. Constitution, the convention in Nevada was sidetracked by a local issue—the controversy over taxation of mines. Proponents of taxation in the Congress and in the Nevada constitutional convention took the position that Nevada's rich mines were located on federal government lands and should therefore be required not only to take out leases but pay royalties on their production. The money would go into the depleted federal treasury. Opponents felt that this form of taxation might kill the territory's flourishing mining industry. The constitutional convention chose to accept the controversial clause imposing the tax on mines.

William Stewart, the man who had persuaded Governor Nye to locate the capital in Carson City, now put his persuasive powers to work again. A strong Union supporter but a stronger opponent of mining taxation, he took his case directly to the people. Nevada's first constitution was defeated, and for a time, it appeared that Lincoln's cause was lost.

The next several months marked the most frenzied period in Nevada's political history. In rapid succession:

—a second convention was elected, and in a four-month period, managed to draft a constitution without the objectionable clause on mining taxation;

—the new constitution was submitted to the people and passed;

—time was of such urgency that the entire document was actually telegraphed to Washington, D.C., at a then staggering cost of $3,416.77;

—acting under authority granted to him by the Congress, President Lincoln officially proclaimed Nevada a state on October 31, 1864.

The activity did not end there. A governor and other state officers, a legislature, and the state's one Congressional representative had to be nominated and elected, and that meant campaigns to be waged. Two U.S. senators, however, had to be chosen by the state legislature, and that meant campaigning of a more personal sort.

Somehow, the task was accomplished. H.G. Blasdel became the first governor of Nevada; H. G. Worthington was elected representative. The duly elected legislature selected James Nye and William Stewart as the first U.S. senators. They rushed to the nation's capital and arrived in time to vote for the Thirteenth Amendment, abolishing slavery. Nevada's debt to the man who had made statehood possible, President Lincoln, was thereby settled.

And the thirty-sixth star in the nation's flag could get on less hurriedly about the proper business of statehood.

In the years that followed, the coming of age of Nevada was predictably marked by the old axiom that there are no immaculate conceptions in the political process. There were times of accord and times of strife, personal triumphs and personal tragedies. Predictably, too, a certain stability and direction were achieved.

The physical boundaries of present-day Nevada were finally defined. The original Territorial Organic Act of 1861 had given Nevada all that part of Utah Territory west of the 116th meridian. Two further slices of Utah were added by acts of Congress in 1862 and 1866, serving to establish most of Nevada's eastern boundary at the expense of ruffled Mormon tempers in the vertical strip. And in 1867, the nibbled triangular piece that is now southern Nevada was annexed from Arizona Territory.

It took a little longer for Nevada to shake off the yoke of a corrupt political system dominated by the Comstock mining tycoons and the "robber barons" of the Central Pacific Railroad. The collapse of the Comstock mining boom in the late years of the ninteenth century did much to accomplish this, at the cost of a devastating blow to Nevada's economy. Almost concurrently, the antiquated system of having the legislature select U.S. senators acclaimed by popular vote—a process shot through with payoffs—was replaced by popular vote in 1913 with the adoption of the Seventeenth Amendment to the U.S. Constitution.

In the wave of voter protest against corruption in politics, Nevada in 1895 enacted an early purity law on elections, requiring candidates to account publicly for all campaign funds received and spent. However, the mechanics of the law proved so difficult that it soon died a natural death and was repealed.

Woman suffrage took even longer to achieve, forty-five years, in fact. Even the speechmaking and peaceful demonstration tactics of suffragette Susan B. Anthony, who came to Nevada to help the cause, failed to break the frontier attitude of male dominance. It was not until 1914 that home-grown Anne Martin managed to win over Governor Tasker Oddie, the legislature, and the voting populace, giving Nevada the dubious distinction of becoming one of the last of the states to approve the ballot for women.

The formative years of territory and statehood saw the making or breaking of an astonishing number of political figures. Only one member of the original territorial government managed to endure for any length of time. He was Territorial Governor James Nye. Most members of the first territorial family had departed in the discouraging period after their arrival. Secretary of State Orion Clemens, who more than any other man had held the territorial government together, failed to become a candidate for that office in the first election after enactment of statehood.

Why this was so remains a puzzle to this day. In positive attributes, Orion Clemens was all that could be desired of a public servant—hard-working, honest, frugal with public funds, and unambitiously content with the position he held. Perhaps he fell victim to the popular erosion that comes to any political man who must make hard decisions and thereby accumulate more enemies than friends. Certainly, it was a failing in him of too much pride. He felt strongly that he had earned the right to be secretary of state, so strongly that he refused to demean himself by appearing at the Republican nominating convention. His reward for that miscalculation was that he was not even named as a candidate.

Orion Clemens sank into instant oblivion. He and his wife remained in Carson City for a short while, probably to be near the grave of their daughter, who had died at the age of ten of spotted fever. When his law practice failed to materialize, he moved first to California and then to Iowa to set up another struggling law practice.

At Orion's death in 1887, Mark Twain—whose remarks had at times been disparaging of his brother's failures—wrote a letter to his widow that was more revealing of Twain's inner torment than of Orion's character. Twain wrote:

> He was good—all good—and sound. There was nothing bad in
> him, nothing base, nor any unkindness. It was unjust that such a
> man . . . should have been sentenced to live seventy-two years. It
> was beautiful, the patience with which he bore it.

As for Territorial Governor James Nye, he at least won election as one of Nevada's first U.S. senators. But even that salvaging of dreams was achieved by the support of William Stewart, Nevada's other first U.S. senator. Nye served as senator from 1865 to 1873, was defeated by John P. Jones, and then went home to New York City and total decline. Nearly friendless and reduced to poverty, he died in an asylum. The contents of his pocket notebook included a pathetic last testament to the standing James Nye once had. It was a handwritten note that read, "Dear General—come up tonight and swap jokes. Lincoln."

The lone, long-lasting political figure to emerge out of Nevada's hectic beginnings was the indomitable William Stewart.

During his twenty-eight-year tenure in the U.S. Senate, inter-
rupted by a ten-year departure from national politics, he was to
become a spokesman for free silver in the international monetary system, sponsor of the first national laws governing mining,
and he aided in drafting the Fifteenth Amendment to the U.S.
Constitution, enfranchising the Negro. It was through Stewart's
influence that Nevada became the first state to ratify the Fifteenth Amendment.

In a little-known interlude in the nation's capital, William
Stewart was to cross paths with the only other early-Nevada figure eventually to win a reputation surpassing his own. Stewart
had known him first as Samuel Clemens, unofficial private secretary to his brother, Orion.

Samuel Clemens had left the company of politics in territorial
days to try his hand at prospecting. That effort having failed ab-
jectly, he tried his hand at reporting under the pen name of
Mark Twain for the *Territorial Enterprise* in Virginia City. In
this endeavor, he fared better as a writer of satire and hoaxes, to
the immense amusement of the populace and at the expense of
any and all prominent citizens pretending to pomposity. Mark
Twain's meandering then led him to California and eventually
to the Holy Land—as a somewhat skeptical pilgrim.

When he returned to the United States, his first order of business was to show up on William Stewart's doorstep with a
demand for employment that would give him time to write
memoirs of his pilgrimage to the Holy Land. Out of old friend-
ship mixed with wary reluctance, Stewart hired Mark Twain as
his secretary. He lived to regret it.

In the temporary absence of his wife and children, Stewart
was living in a boarding house operated by a prim and proper
spinster. Mark Twain moved in and promptly proceeded to
make life a nightmare for the spinster with a slouching demeanor and an affected menacing attitude designed only to ter-
rify her. He succeeded to the point that Stewart threatened to
thrash him if he persisted in frightening the poor woman.

On the heels of this episode, Stewart made the mistake of
leaving the capital and entrusting the affairs of his office to
Mark Twain. When Stewart returned, his political relationships
were in a shambles. In Stewart's absence, Mark Twain had

taken it upon himself to write several letters answering requests from Stewart's constituents in Nevada.

One of the requests was from the citizenry of a settlement called Baldwin's Ranch, asking with extreme politeness for Senator Stewart's help in providing a post office for the community.

Mark Twain's answer read:

> What the mischief do you suppose you want with a post office at Baldwin's Ranch? It would not do you any good. If any letters came there, you couldn't read them, you know; and besides, such letters as ought to pass through, with money in them, for other localities, would not be like to get through, you must perceive at once; and that would make trouble for us all. No, don't bother about a post office in your camp. I have your best interests at heart, and feel that it would only be an ornamental folly. What you want is a jail, you know—a nice substantial jail and a free school. These will be a lasting benefit to you. These will make you really contented and happy. I will move in the matter at once.
>
> Mark Twain.
> For William M. Stewart,
> U.S. Senator.

Stewart in near-apoplexy waved the letter and its reply— threatening to hang Stewart if he ever entered that district again—in Mark Twain's face, and fired him on the spot. Twain promised to get even with him, which he did. When later he wrote *Roughing It*—a humorous memoir of his adventures in the West—he said that Stewart had swindled him in a mining deal. And included a portrait of Stewart with a pirate's patch over one eye.

But first, Mark Twain completed the book he had begun writing in his brief time with Stewart, the book that was to launch him as one of the immortals of American literature. It was called *The Innocents Abroad*.

9

Exploits Great and Small

*T*HE day of the Comstock lode and the few years preceding it remain unequaled in Nevada history for the number of folk heroes they produced. In the amalgam of humanity that the westward movement had thrown together, valiant deeds and violent deeds went hand in hand.

It did not seem to matter whether the men and women who performed them were good or bad. In the curious ambivalence of frontier life, they were boasted about with the same measure of pride. The fact that they were Nevada's own overrode other considerations.

This attitude by chroniclers and citizenry alike led, of course, to all sorts of exaggeration. If a gunfighter had in reality killed only two men, his score was inevitably boosted in the telling. If a prostitute caught the public fancy, she was endowed with all the instincts of a saint.

A man named Snowshoe Thompson was one of those cast in the truly heroic mould, with a giant frame and courage to fit it. A Norwegian who had come to California in the gold rush and Nevada in the silver rush, he became an instant legend as a mail carrier over the snowbound winter Sierra. Until he arrived upon the scene, mail service between western Nevada and northern California was almost nonexistent. A few men had ventured the winter passage on webbed snowshoes as we know them today. But the task proved to be too arduous and dangerous, and there were long periods of time when Nevada simply went without news from the nearest centers of civilization.

Recalling the skis of his childhood, Thompson fashioned what he called a Norwegian snowshoe. Hence the nickname he acquired. Made out of fir planking, his skis were ten feet long, five inches wide, and nearly two inches thick at their center of balance. Only a man with prodigious strength could have climbed mountains with such ponderous contraptions on his feet and a mailbag weighing sixty to eighty pounds on his back.

Snowshoe Thompson was such a man. For three long winters, he carried the mail between Genoa in western Nevada and Placerville in California's mother-lode country. The one-hundred-eighty-mile round trip took him from three to five days, depending upon the severity of storms. With neither overcoat nor blanket, he traveled day and night, stopping only for short periods of rest or for refuge from blizzards. In these pauses, he would find dead stumps of pine and set fire to them to keep from freezing to death. It was said of him that he never lost his way through deep forests and the wildest of storms.

Finally, however, exhaustion took its toll and his giant strength abandoned him. He fell sick and died before he was yet fifty years old, leaving behind him an heroic legend and a grave in Genoa, which has become a shrine of the modern ski world.

When the Comstock lode was struck, another kind of folk hero was to emerge out of the early days of Virginia City. He was a product of lawless times and an almost unanimous dislike for Wells Fargo's exorbitant rates for travel and shipping.

Robbing of Wells Fargo stages leaving Virginia City with bullion became almost a ritual. At some turn on a lonely road, the stage driver would be confronted with an obstacle such as a small tree or boulder lying across the path, and behind it, masked men armed with shotguns. Since the stage driver did not consider the fighting off of bandits as part of his job, he would throw down the strongbox and go on his way.

Few tears were shed in a community that regarded the holdup as a dispute between masked robbers and corporate robbers. It was an open secret that the highwaymen had spies in express offices to alert them when bullion was being shipped. And one stage driver was held up so often that he was widely suspected of being on the bandits' payroll.

Out of this state of affairs was born a host of romantic stories about the highwaymen of the Comstock lode. The most romantic concerned an episode that was supposed to have occurred on the Geiger Grade approach to Virginia City. Two Wells Fargo stages traveling as a team were held up by seven masked highwaymen. When the passengers descended from their coaches, the highwaymen were pleasantly surprised to find that the boot of one stagecoach was filled with champagne and gourmet delicacies. Also, that there were ladies aboard.

When the business at hand was completed—namely, relieving the other coach of its strongbox and the passengers of their jewelry and money—a feast was prepared. Rugs were spread on the ground for the ladies, and passengers and highwaymen alike partook of champagne and edibles before going their separate ways.

Of all the Comstock's highwaymen, Jack Davis was the most famous. He was said to be a man of such mild demeanor that he could have passed for a clergyman. His company was much sought after, and he often played at cards with the very men whose bullion he had stolen the day before.

Jack Davis never admitted to being a highwayman. As a front, he owned a mill in Six-Mile Canyon below Virginia City. It was a remarkable mill. No ore was ever seen making its way to the mill, but nevertheless the mill managed to produce a steady stream of bullion that looked suspiciously remelted. Also noteworthy was the fact that not one of Jack Davis's shipments of bullion to San Francisco was ever robbed.

The coming of the railroads was a severe blow to the highwaymen's lucrative way of life. In the Comstock, the blow was particularly severe when the Virginia and Truckee shortline made a connecting link with the Central Pacific Railroad in Reno. All that mass of metal and steam and momentum seemed to spell the end of bandit rule of the roads. It was left to Jack Davis to ponder the dilemma and come up with a solution.

So, on November 1, 1870, what was hailed as the first train robbery in American history took place at the Verdi station near

Reno. Masked men led by a mild-mannered bandit relieved the train of $40,000 in gold coin contained, of course, in a Wells Fargo strongbox. And on that note, Jack Davis retired to respectability.

In Virginia City's rowdy times, the breed known alternately as gunfighter, man-eater, desperado, and desperate scoundrel, was regarded as a cut below the highwaymen. It included such personalities as Rattlesnake Dick, Red-Handed Mike, Blue Dick, Cut-Mouth Burke, and Fighting Sam Brown. These men never attained the status of folk hero. In Virginia City's relative way of looking at things, they were relegated to the class of cut-throat.

Others of the gunfighting ilk, however, managed to attain fame and admiration of sorts. One was a quiet gambler, Langford ("Farmer") Peel, a man regarded as so dangerous that other "chiefs" of the Comstock would go to any lengths to avoid a quarrel with him. Rumor had it that he had killed five men before coming to Virginia City. Although this may have been exaggerated, one thing was certain. Farmer Peel was no stranger to the business of man killing.

The most macabre of his gunfights in Virginia City came about when a "freshcomer" named El Dorado Johnny rode into town with the avowed intent of killing Farmer Peel and thereby earning himself a reputation. Before confronting Peel, El Dorado Johnny went to a barbershop for a shave, hair-curl, and a boot polish "so that he would look nice" in the event he came out second best. His prettying efforts were not wasted. He walked into the saloon that was Farmer Peel's favorite hangout and taunted him. Peel took up the challenge, invited El Dorado Johnny into the street, and killed him with one shot.

Although he lost face by it, Farmer Peel figured in another incident that probably went a long way in establishing him as a "gentleman" gunfighter with the stuff of heroes. There was a contemporary of Mark Twain on the staff of the *Territorial Enterprise*. His name was William Wright, but he wrote under the pen name of Dan De Quille. Like Twain, he was a beginning reporter with no great reputation.

By nature, Dan De Quille was shy and retiring, but still a

courageous reporter. In a newspaper story, he described one of Farmer Peel's shooting frays in a tone that was not complimentary to the gunfighter. Peel threatened vengeance, which was chilling news in a day when reporters and editors alike often feared for their lives when reporting the violent news of Virginia City.

With cause, Dan De Quille was frightened. Nevertheless, he chose to confront Farmer Peel, searching him out in a saloon.

"I hear you are looking for me," said De Quille.

A tense moment passed as Farmer Peel regarded the slender young reporter. Obviously impressed by De Quille's quiet courage, Peel said, "Well, I have read your story again and it is mainly accurate. I have no complaints." Then, as the story goes, he invited De Quille to have a drink with him.

Not long afterwards, Farmer Peel took his leave of Virginia City. He wandered to other mining camps and finally to Helena, Montana, where he was killed in a gunfight. It was a fate he shared with Western gunfighters whose violent way of life never permitted them to live past their youth.

The most enigmatic of Virginia City's parade of badmen was Tom Peasley. Though he was cast early into the role of a dangerous man, Tom Peasley seemed always to be yearning for respectability. In a time when most arguments were settled by bushwhacking an enemy, Peasley insisted on a fair fight, which usually amounted to a walkdown duel in plain sight of everyone. Because of their rarity, such tactics were hailed as the ultimate in fair play. But even in this, Peasley was to be frustrated.

In his next to last gunfight, Peasley shot down one Sugarfoot Jack Jenkins. To the public's amazement and to his own private horror, Peasley discovered that Sugarfoot Jack had gone through all the motions of a fight except one, that of arming himself. After that, Peasley made it known that he was finished with violence. He became respectable to the point where he was named sergeant-at-arms of the legislative senate in Carson City, in 1865.

Tall and powerful and given to rough horseplay, Peasley mistook a stranger named Tom Barnhart for a friend and knocked him to his knees with an overaffectionate slap on the back. Peasley apologized, but Barnhart took the incident to heart.

One winter night while Tom Peasley and his newfound respectable friends were sitting around a potbellied stove in Carson City's Ormsby House, Barnhart approached them from a cardroom with drawn gun.

"You don't mean to shoot me, do you?" Peasley called out incredulously.

In answer, Barnhart shot him twice in the chest. Mortally wounded, Tom Peasley rose from his chair and drew his own gun. Barnhart fled into the cardroom. Peasley staggered after him, braced himself in the doorway, and emptied his gun into the fleeing figure. Then Peasley collapsed from his own wounds. His last whispered plea was that his boots be taken off so that he could die like a respectable man.

Not all the incidents of lawlessness during the Comstock era had such a grim ending. Many were laced with humor, and one in particular made for much laughter among the male gentry of western Nevada.

A flamboyant gambler named Billy Mayfield had been sentenced to prison for stabbing a sheriff. The prison was a makeshift affair that had once been a territorial hostelry situated near Carson City. Its warden was Abraham Curry, a kindly man who was reluctant to put locks on rooms that passed for cells. Since gambler Billy Mayfield was one of the prison's first inmates, and the very first escapee, Warden Curry was reluctant to explain how the escape had come about.

The mystery was cleared up by Billy Mayfield's flair for publicity. He wrote a letter to the *Territorial Enterprise* in Virginia City. It read, in best part:

> The guard was walking back and forth in the ward room, while old man Curry was sitting playing poker with some of the workhands about ten feet from my cell. I got down on my knees, and watching the old man's eyes, started for the door. As I got to it, I saw the old man raising the hand that had just been dealt to him, and, as his eyes were directed toward me, I thought I would wait until he got a big hand, for, being an old gambler myself, I knew it would always excite an unsophisticated gambler to have a high

hand dealt to him. A few minutes afterward, a big Irishman who was playing in the game got a big hand, queens and sevens, before the draw. He bet "twenty beans." The old man saw it, and they took one card each. The old man drew a king, making him a king full; the Irishman drew a queen, making him a queen full. They bet and bet until they had about two hundred beans in the pot. All this time I was fixing to go, and I came to the conclusion that if I couldn't go out on that hand, I never could, and so I went.

Two years and some months after statehood and its seeming mantle of respectability, Virginia City scandalized the nation by staging a lavish funeral for a prostitute.

In January of 1867, the body of Julia Bulette was found in Virginia City's red-light district. She had been strangled in her crib. Her jewels, furs, and clothing had been stolen.

News of the sultry Creole's murder created more than an ordinary stir among the male populace of the Comstock. In her time in Virginia City, Julia Bulette had not only acquired jewels and furs, but also station. She had, in fact, been elected to honorary membership in the local fire department. Since the fire department constituted one of the most select social groups in Virginia City, this was no mean feat.

An intensive search was launched for her murderer. At the same time, stories of the courtesan's kindnesses to unemployed miners were magnified to the point of legend. The fire department took up a collection for an elaborate casket and a finely engraved tombstone. That much tribute would have been acceptable to the proper women of Virginia City. But not what followed.

Funeral services were conducted in one of the engine houses, to an overflow crowd of male citizens from all walks of life. The funeral procession through Virginia City to Flowery Hill cemetery included carriages filled with men in their Sunday best and prostitutes in black, members of the fire department marching in full uniform, and a brass band. The proper women of Virginia City pulled down their shades as the procession passed.

When Julia Bulette's suspected murderer was captured, however, the women had their revenge. Until the day he was "hung," Jean Millain never went a day without cakes and pies and comforts of all kinds. It goes without saying that his dark, handsome looks added to the women's retribution and to their husbands' chagrin.

The story of the Comstock's first millionaire and his wife was of the rags-to-riches substance of which every fortune seeker dreamed.

Sandy Bowers was an unlettered working miner who managed to save enough of his wages to buy a small claim in Gold Hill on the outskirts of Virginia City. He lived in a boarding-house operated by Eilley Orrum, a hard-working woman who cooked meals and washed clothes for her boarders. When one of them could not pay his bill, he blithely signed away a small mining claim that he owned. By coincidence, the claim happened to adjoin that of Sandy Bowers. This fact of neighboring claims prompted the boarders to the perpetration of a good joke—urging Sandy Bowers to marry Eilley Orrum. He did so, and, as predicted, the union caused much amusement among the miners. They did not laugh quite so hard when rich deposits of gold and silver were found on the two claims.

Money poured into the laps of slow-witted Sandy Bowers and his wife in such quantity that at first they did not know what to do with it. They soon learned. After buying a new home and attiring themselves in fine clothes, they decided to build a mansion in the verdant valley that lay between the Virginia Mountains and the Sierra. While it was being erected, Sandy and Eilley yielded to the advice of their practical-joker friends that they should go to Europe to get "polished" enough to live up to their new station in life. And while they were there, they should drop in on the queen of England.

Sandy and Eilley never got to see the queen, but they saw practically everything else. They also went on a spending spree for their new mansion. Ornate furniture, fireplaces of Italian marble, chandeliers and mirrors from France, all made their way by boat to San Francisco and then by wagon over the Sierra.

Sandy Bowers, at least, tasted the full fruits of his fortune. Bowers's mansion in Washoe Valley became the setting for the fanciest parties Nevada has probably ever known. At the Bowerses' expense, caravans of fine carriages made their way down from Virginia City to banquets and balls at the mansion. Imported wines, French champagne, seafood from the Pacific Ocean, orchestras, and liveried servants were all part of the grand display.

And then, Sandy Bowers died, and the swindlers and the cheaters descended upon Eilley to strip her of her fortune. Her mine and mill went into debt, and she was left with nothing but a silent, unwanted mansion in which to eke out her remaining years. For Eilley Orrum Bowers, her Nevada adventure had come full circle from rags to riches to rags.

Each in his own way, the folk heroes managed to leave indelible imprints on the character of Nevada. In some curious way their lives and deeds—heroic and not so heroic—were to be repeated in other times and settings in history yet to be made.

10

Titans of Nevada Politics

"It was the first political rally I had ever gone to. I was just a kid then, but I remember it well. The old American Legion Hall was filled with mothball-smelling suits of miners come to town, buckaroos reeking with whiskey, Indians and the bitter smell of sagebrush, and the hard, unwashed sweat of working men that really mounted up to something by the Friday before the Saturday-night bath.

"Senator Pittman was standing on a stage that was absolutely dazzling with red, white, and blue bunting and flags and huge swatches of butcher paper bearing his name and that of the Democratic party. He was a slender man with a fine face and bearing. But at the moment, he was having some trouble with his bearing. Every time he made a grand gesture with one hand, he had to reach out with the other and hold on to a table that wobbled. The senator was talking about silver, but that didn't interest me at all. I was fascinated instead by that table's spindly legs and what would happen if they suddenly collapsed under the senator's hand. It was torture for me, because I wanted it to happen and not to happen, because I knew this man was proud.

"I was released from my dilemma by an incident that diminished the affair of the table. The senator made one flourish grander than the rest, and his coat burst open in front. There as plain as day showed the butt end of a pistol stuck in his waist-

band. But the senator wasn't embarrassed one bit. 'Ladies and gentlemen,' he said. 'You have nothing to fear, because you are my friends. I have carried this piece of hardware from the time I was a boy in the Deep South until I became a man in the hard life of the Klondike. And I will continue to carry it until my dying day, because a man in politics is not without enemies.'

"Then the senator laughed and said in that rich drawl of his, 'Anyway, I am the one who is taking the risk. Because if that thing should ever go off, its business end canted the way it is, I will never be the man I was before.' And the women covered their faces with scandalized pleasure and the men stomped their feet and shook the hall with their laughing."

"Senator McCarran was a man you had a lot of respect for, or none. If he was your enemy, you knew you had one. He played politics the way it should be played, rough and tumble, but clean with no duplicity. He had an Irish quality of humor and wildness and moodiness. He never forgot a stab in the back, and he waited until he could settle the score. Then he would open his arms and say, 'Let's start over.'

"He was a goodhearted man, but he would fight you in a minute. You know, you appreciate a man like that."

"Pat McCarran distrusted peace and quiet. He considered it an apathetic state of mind, and a sign that the country wasn't going anywhere. He believed you never got anything without fighting for it. He loved to fight. It lighted up his whole day. And he fought them all—FDR, Harold Ickes, Harry Truman, Dean Acheson, Henry Wallace. Roosevelt didn't know what to make of him. McCarran fought him on his try to pack the Supreme Court and McCarran won. And then McCarran would turn around and support him on the next issue. Roosevelt went so far as to stump Nevada to get McCarran beat. He was not very successful.

"He created the Senate Internal Security Subcommittee only to awaken the people on the Communist threat. He never anticipated that Joe McCarthy, who was not even a member of the

subcommittee, would turn it into a nightmare. He told McCarthy that if he distorted the findings of the subcommittee to go after Communists, he was digging his own grave. He admired McCarthy for his courage and believed him to be a dedicated American, but he thought McCarthy had poor judgment—going about a good thing in the wrong way. He told McCarthy time and again, 'Be judicial, Joe. You are persecuting individuals on shaky grounds.' But McCarthy chose not to listen, and for a while McCarran quit speaking to him. In the end, he stuck by McCarthy because of loyalty. That was McCarran's greatest strength and his greatest weakness. He thought loyalty was the only quality that counted in a man.''

"Pat McCarran never forgot a favor. Once, when he was a young man, he got drunk in a mining-camp saloon and, as was his Irish habit, managed to clean out the place. Instead of throwing Pat in jail, the old sheriff took him home and had the wife cook up a supper to sober him up, and then they put him to bed. Years later, when McCarran was chairman of the Senate Judiciary Committee, a federal judgeship vacancy came up in San Francisco. The local bar association made its customary recommendation to fill the judgeship. McCarran told them, 'The son of my old friend is a superior-court judge out there, and I think he should have it.' The bar association refused to go along. McCarran said, 'Well, in that case, I don't think there'll be any federal judges appointed anywhere in the United States for a while.' And, by God, he didn't call a meeting of the judiciary committee for three months. By that time, the pressure got so great on the bar association that it finally backed down. The federal judgeship went to the son of McCarran's old friend, which friend, as it turned out, was the small-town sheriff who had done McCarran a good turn in the early days.''

"McCarran was so powerful he could introduce a bill calling for the execution of the president and get twenty votes.''

ILLIAM STEWART. Key Pittman. Patrick McCarran. Three men who rank as the unquestioned giants of Nevada politics from first statehood until McCarran's death in 1954. Among them, they served Nevada in the U.S. Senate for seventy-seven years.

Though all three men were markedly different in their approach to politics, they nevertheless shared many common ingredients that have—consciously or unconsciously—been handed down to later generations of Nevada politicians.

The foremost ingredient was that of strong individualism. In the long run, it seemed to matter little to the voters what their senators believed in, as long as they believed in something, were willing to stand by it, and were therefore predictable in their performance in office. The vacillating or the intellectually dilettante politician has rarely been successful in Nevada politics. Probably the only exception to this was Francis G. Newlands, who served three terms in the U. S. Senate after election in 1903. Newlands authored the National Reclamation Act. His "eastern ways," however, did not make much of an impact on the homefolks.

The second ingredient, at least in the formative years, was that of frontier exposure. It did not matter whether it was Nevada frontier, as long as it was frontier of some kind. William Stewart had come directly from the California gold rush to the Nevada silver rush. Key Pittman had come from the Klondike to the Tonopah strike. And Patrick McCarran was reared as the son of a Nevada sheep rancher. It was in McCarran's time that the distinction of "native son" became a political advantage that was to hold sway for many years.

Of the three men, William Stewart was probably the most clever politician. In spite of the handicap of a fiery temper, he was a master in the art of alternative. If he could not accomplish his end by one means, he did it by another. Key Pittman's strength lay in his gracious Southern manner, which so endeared him to voters that he never faced a serious contest. His personal peccadilloes of liking strong drink and carrying a pistol were shrugged off as part of his individualism. McCarran's strength lay in his direct approach to everything. Though he could be ruthless to his enemies, he was fiercely loyal to his friends. And this, too, came to be regarded by the voters as part of his individual appeal.

William Stewart's twenty-nine-year tenure in the U.S. Senate was drawing to a close when young, Southern-born Key Pittman drifted into the new boom camp of Tonopah in 1902. His route had been somewhat circuitous. Having been drawn first to the Klondike gold rush and finding no riches, he came to try his hand in Nevada. He was eminently successful, but as a lawyer instead of a miner. In no time at all, his knowledge of mining law won him his belated fortune. That goal having been satisfied, he turned his interests and oratorical bent to politics.

Key Pittman's entry into state politics seemed at first to be a mixed blessing. In 1910 he challenged incumbent U.S. Senator George Nixon. This was in the transitional period when U.S. senators were still selected by the state legislature. However, the candidates were also required to stand for election by vote of the people. The popular vote was intended to serve as a mandate upon the legislature.

Incumbent Senator Nixon, a Republican, won the popular vote, which should have insured perfunctory approval by the legislature. The only hitch was that a majority of Democrats was simultaneously elected to the legislature, thus opening the door to Pittman's selection by Democratic colleagues as U.S. senator. Despite immense party pressures, Pittman put a stop to the political shenanigans by accepting the popular vote and therefore, defeat.

Though it did not seem so at the time, this gracious act was to reap enduring rewards. When Senator Nixon died two years later, Key Pittman won election in 1912 by the state legislature to fill the vacancy. Throughout his long tenure as U.S. senator, Pittman was never again to be seriously challenged.

At the apex of his career, Key Pittman was regarded by many observers as one of the most influential men in the Congress. Always a champion of free coinage of silver—which was vital to Nevada's precarious economy—he scored his greatest coup in the post-World War I period. His Pittman Act required the federal government to buy millions of ounces of silver needed to help England at one dollar an ounce, a prodigious increase from the existing price of fifty-nine cents an ounce. Though the Pittman Act lasted only from 1918 to 1923, it was to provide a great stimulus to silver mining in the western states.

Key Pittman came to be recognized as an expert in monetary affairs. In 1933, President Franklin D. Roosevelt named him as one of the United States' emissaries to a worldwide financial conference in London. There, he was instrumental in drafting an international agreement raising the price of silver, for which he was praised. He also shot out some London streetlights one night, for which he was not praised.

The years preceding World War II proved to be the most trying of Key Pittman's career. As chairman of the foreign relations committee, he was adamant that the United States should remain neutral. He carried his conviction to the point of calling for an embargo on arms to any foreign nation. Then, as the world drifted inexorably into war, he made a wrenching personal decision and publicly changed his stand. He still stood his ground on opposing American involvement in foreign conflicts. Yet he was one of the first to sound a warning on the Japanese menace in the Pacific. He was not to live to see his prophecy come true. In 1940, five days after he had been elected to his sixth term in office, he died.

In contrast to Key Pittman's graceful advent into Nevada politics, and his tenure thereafter, the career of Patrick McCarran was always a stormy one. As a ragged schoolboy who rode ten miles on horseback to get to a country schoolhouse near Reno, McCarran was in a fistfight nearly every day. One of his early schoolteachers recalled, "The other kids couldn't feel sorry for him, because he wasn't the kind you felt sorry for. So they fought him."

McCarran was one of the last of Nevada's "saddleback lawyers," learning his law while herding sheep, from books stuffed into a packbag, developing oratorical skill by standing on a rock and delivering speeches to an uninterested band of grazing sheep.

In personal appearance, McCarran was stocky in build with a deep chest and powerful arms from his arduous, outdoors youth. His trademark in later years was his leonine mane of silver hair, of which he was so extraordinarily vain that he refused to wear a hat.

In the beginning, his political promise was sporadic. Though he served alternately as a state legislator, district attorney, and a state supreme court justice, he was soundly beaten in two attempts at the U.S. Senate. On the third time around, the Great Depression and the Roosevelt landslide were the only factors that swept him into office over Republican incumbent Tasker Oddie in 1932.

McCarran had hardly been seated as a U.S. senator when he committed political heresy. To the astonishment of his colleagues and the wrath of a goodly part of the nation—excepting, of course, Nevada—he rose on the Senate floor to attack the New Deal policies of President Roosevelt. It remains a moot point whether McCarran's action was motivated by self-aggrandizement or sincere personal conviction.

In any case, McCarran from that day forward was locked in battle on more occasions than not with Roosevelt, and certainly sprang to national attention as a maverick solon. A conservative and an isolationist, he opposed the draft and lend-lease, national health insurance, and federal aid to education. Later, he tempered his views. His greatest victory over the president was in successfully leading the Senate battle against Roosevelt's so-called packing of the U.S. Supreme Court. For that, he was placed on Roosevelt's purge list, a removal attempt that predictably failed with the voters of Nevada.

McCarran was not a negativist, however. He sponsored the Civil Aeronautics Act of 1938 and the important Administrative Procedures Act of 1946. The latter act stripped major federal agencies such as the Federal Communications Commission of their power to act as both prosecutor and judge in instances of alleged violation of government rules. He sponsored numerous mining-subsidy bills, protected the rights of cattlemen and sheepmen, and was a champion of labor. Always, the welfare of Nevada was his first priority. At one point he was accused by his enemies in Washington of "sacking the federal treasury" in his efforts to help Nevada. This accusation was not as outlandish as it seemed. In 1948, for example, Nevada paid $41 million in federal income taxes and received federal projects costing $175 million.

In his twenty-one-year tenure in the U.S. Senate, McCarran rose to a stature equalling that of Key Pittman. But where Key Pittman was regarded as a reasoned man of influence, McCarran was regarded as a man with a penchant for power. And power was a weapon that McCarran was not at all reluctant to wield.

He became chairman of the Senate Judiciary Committee and a ranking member of the Appropriations Committee. As a result of these two positions, he controlled much of the legislation that passed through Congress.

His most trying time in office came during consideration of the McCarran-Walter Immigration Act, which was roundly attacked by eastern liberals as discriminatory to Hungarians and Poles. McCarran felt that immigrants from the Soviet orbit included numbers of hidden Communists. On the merits of the act itself, he protested that it was in fact a codification of court rulings on immigrant cases, and that he would be the first to offer amendments if time proved the need.

Nevertheless, he was personally troubled by the bill, since it involved denial of immigration to many Catholics behind the Iron Curtain, and he was a rigid Catholic himself. He was summoned by the Vatican to hear objections to the bill, and dutifully answered the call. When he returned, McCarran was in turmoil. He confided to a friend, "I have just doomed myself to purgatory. I have defied the Pope."

On the home front in Nevada, however, McCarran was very nearly unassailable. Part of the reason was that he never forgot his constituency. It was a rule of his office that any letter from a Nevadan must be answered the same day it was received, and some kind of action taken on it the day afterward. He dispensed thousands of favors to the so-called little people from which he had come.

One favor so rendered has become legend. The owner of a sprawling cattle ranch in northeastern Nevada received a telephone call one day from McCarran in Washington. "You got any wood on that ranch?" McCarran asked. "What do you mean, wood?" the rancher said. "I mean firewood," McCarran said. "Hell, I guess so," the rancher said. "Well, do me a favor," McCarran said. "There's a miner up Tuscarora Canyon who broke his chopping arm and can't get in his winter wood. Would you take a couple of truckloads up for him?"

No wonder then that when McCarran dropped dead of a heart attack in 1954, his funeral in Reno was attended not only by men of high station and great wealth, but by hundreds of his little people—prospectors, sheepherders, buckaroos, and working men. The smell of mothballs was everywhere.

The passing of Senator Patrick McCarran is said to have signalled the end of the rough-hewn era of Nevada politics, and ushered in a different breed of politician and a change in Nevadans' voting habits. Under scrutiny, however, this belief does not stand up.

The politician of today may possess more sophistication in the tactics of modern campaigning. But that skill amounts more to an ability to adapt to the times. It does not touch on the enduring substance of the classic Nevada politician.

Strong individualism in a candidate is still a requisite for success. Graciousness in manner is still expected, and eloquence with the spoken word is still admired. The Lincolnesque touch of rude beginnings is no handicap whatever. And the candidate who can claim a colorful past is at an advantage over a more sheltered opponent.

As for Nevadans' voting habits, they have remained remarkably constant since first statehood. Even the presence of a substantial transient population in the metropolitan centers of Las Vegas and Reno is not altogether that different from times past. With its history of mining rushes and subsequent population exoduses, Nevada has always had its goodly share of transients. And, in many cases, transients have a habit of seeking advice from long-standing locals as to the best man for the job.

Other patterns are revealing. Nevadans with rare exception choose lawyers in the tradition of Stewart, Pittman, and McCarran, to represent them in the halls of Congress. And they hold on to their senators and representatives. In recent times, for example, U.S. Senator Alan Bible remained in office for twenty years before his retirement in 1974. And Congressman Walter Baring, a "maverick" Democrat nearly always at odds with his party, also held office for twenty years. The only man to hold all three major offices—governor, congressman, senator—was James G. Scrugham, a professor-historian who fathered the state park system.

Conversely, Nevadans elect most of their governors from a wide variety of occupations other than the law. In the early years of statehood, mining men, businessmen, and ranchers predominated in the role of chief executive. The first elected governor, Henry Goode Blasdel, was a mining man who, incidentally, almost perished on a trek to view firsthand the mining strikes and Mormon agriculture in southern Nevada. He and his party got lost in the deserts. One man died, and the remainder had to subsist for days on lizards.

Blasdel was followed by Lewis ("Old Broadhorns") Bradley, the man who drove the first longhorn cattle to Nevada. Bradley, was followed, in turn, by John Kinkead, another mining man. And so on until 1911, when Tasker Oddie became the first lawyer to fill the office of governor. Even then, Oddie was better known as a mining man who had been involved in the silver and gold strikes of Tonopah and Goldfield. Oddie also had a colorful interlude in his life. When claim jumpers threatened to take over the rich strikes owned by him and his partners, Oddie hired no less than former Tombstone Marshal Wyatt Earp to guard their rights.

In the varied occupations from which Nevada has drawn its governors, only two newspaper publishers have been elected. They were Vail Pittman, brother of U.S. Senator Key Pittman, who served from 1945 to 1951, and Charles Russell, who served from 1951 to 1959. They were followed by two lawyers: Grant Sawyer, who served from 1959 to 1967, and Paul Laxalt, who served from 1967 to 1971. The latter was followed by Mike O'Callaghan, schoolteacher and Job Corps administrator and war hero who lost a leg in the Korean conflict. With his practice of telephoning constituents without going through his secretary, Governor O'Callaghan achieved a reputation for familiarity reminiscent of Patrick McCarran.

Another tendency in the traditional pattern of Nevada politics is that of choosing its chief executives from those candidates who had residence or roots in the state's small towns. Governors through nearly four decades have either come from the small towns of Nevada or had early family roots there. Governor E. P. Carville, who served from 1939 to 1945, was originally from Mound Valley in northeastern Nevada; Vail Pittman was an undersheriff in Tonopah in his youth; Charles Russell was from Deeth in northeastern Nevada; Grant Sawyer was a small-town district attorney in Elko; Paul Laxalt was a district attorney in Carson City; and Mike O'Callaghan had been a schoolteacher in the industrial town of Henderson near Las Vegas.

A penchant for voting "for the man and not the party" has been another distinguishing feature of Nevada politics. Democrats have outnumbered Republicans since the depression and its consequent ousting of Republicans from all major offices. In recent years, Democratic registration has reached nearly a two-to-one superiority over Republicans. Yet, Republicans manage to get elected to the high posts of governor, U.S. senator, and U.S. representative. Two of Nevada's last four governors, Charles Russell and Paul Laxalt, were Republican candidates. Two of Nevada's last four elected U.S. senators—George Malone and Paul Laxalt—were Republican candidates. And two of Nevada's last four representatives in Congress, Clifton Young and David Towell, were Republican candidates.

In the uncertain game that is politics, this bolting of party lines can probably be traced to two things. One is an old Nevada habit of coppering political bets. Nevadans traditionally have been uncomfortable with the prospect of one-party domination. So, in nearly every election for major office, at least one Republican can be assured of challenging successfully an overwhelming Democratic registration.

The other reason, of course, is the candidate himself. Nevada's population is still small enough that most voters can get to know their candidates personally, and weigh them accordingly. This is particularly true in the state's small counties, which have often proved to be the deciding factor in a standoff between Reno and environs in the north and Las Vegas and its environs in the south. In these regions of old Nevada, familiarity with candidates extends to calling governors, U.S. senators, and representatives by their first names. From the beginning, being singularly unimpressed with titles has been the distinguishing trait of Nevada's small counties.

In the metropolitan centers of Las Vegas and Reno, however, the rapid growth in numbers of people has eroded the institution of voter-knowing-candidate and vice versa. More and more, politicians in statewide races are having to rely on media, especially television, to achieve the campaign ideal of "name identification."

By religious denomination, the two major cohesive voting blocs are Catholics and Mormons. Mormons dominate in southern Nevada, and Catholics throughout the rest of the state. Yet, even these unified voting blocs have recently shown signs of breaking down in political preference. Though U.S. Senator Howard Cannon of Las Vegas is a Mormon who can count on heavy Mormon support, it is not unusual for Mormon leaders to splinter off, aligning themselves against other Mormon candidates. And solid Catholic support of a Catholic candidate is also breaking down.

The same diffusion applies to organized labor. Nevada is a right-to-work state, and Nevadans have voted down all attempts at compulsory unionism. Surprisingly, the defenders of right-to-work have found support at the polls from a substantial number of rank-and-file union members. And political candidates who have not won endorsement at AFL-CIO meetings of union leaders have also found that organized labor's vote is not all that regimented.

Almost to a man, candidates for statewide races have decried the existence of sectionalism in Nevada. For the most part, this is predictable political strategy for candidates who must draw support both from heavily populated Las Vegas and Clark County in the south and Reno and smaller counties to the north.

However, Nevada's small counties in particular still harbor a deep suspicion of the Las Vegas scene. This is natural from a circumstance of staid old communities confronted with the newly arrived phenomenon of Las Vegas. It will be a long time breaking down.

A century and more of statehood has brought shiftings of political situations and alliances, but the basic ingredient for success in Nevada politics comes back to where it has always been—the personal worth of the candidate himself and the independent attitudes of Nevadans themselves. There is much of Missouri "show me" in the sagebrush state.

11

The Melting Pot

"You would call it a real international settlement these days, but there were some other words, not so nice, for it then. It was a copper company town, and the whole population only amounted to a few thousand people. But, Jesus, was it divided! There was Greek Town, Hunky Town, Jap Town, Wop Town, and Mid Town. That meant the middle of town, and it was where all the 'white people' lived. The rest of us were cheap labor for the copper mines and the smelter. The 'foreigners' stuck together for the most part, but once in a while, you could get a scrap if you were a Hunky and you crossed the line into Greek Town. Our common enemy was Mid Town. Anytime you crossed that line, you were in for big trouble. I was a Serb, and my mother had a cow in Hunky Town. It was my job to sell milk to houses in Mid Town. The first couple of times, I went alone. And sure enough, there would be a gang of 'white' kids waiting for me. They would take the milk pail away from me and spill it on the ground, and then they would beat me up. So I went to my father and said 'I am tired of getting beat up because I'm a Hunky.' And he said, 'I don't care how many times you get beat up. You are a Serb and you got to be proud of it. If I ever hear of you running away from a fight, you will get a worse beating from me than them.' So I went back and I got beat up a thousand times, but I won a few, too, when I could get some of my Hunky friends to go with me.

"*Then a funny thing happened. When we got into high school, we were all together–'whites' and 'foreigners' alike. When the 'foreigners' showed they were good at sports, the people in Mid Town began to look at us differently. And when we won a few state championships, it changed altogether. That was when all the barriers broke down. They finally accepted us as human.*

"*I guess it's the way life is, but now I go back there and some of my best friends are the guys from Mid Town. We can laugh about it now, but it was sure nothing to laugh about then.*"

"*All of us together were of a generation born of old-country people who spoke English with an accent and prayed in another language, who drank red wine and cooked their food in the old-country way, and peeled apples and pears after dinner.*

"*We were among the last whose names would tell our blood and the kind of faces we had, to know another language in our homes, to suffer youthful shame because of that language and refuse to speak it, and a later shame because of what we had done, and hurt because we had caused a hurt so deep it could never find words.*

"*And the irony of it was that our mothers and fathers were truer Americans than we, because they had forsaken home and family, and gone into the unknown of a new land with only courage and the hands that God gave them, and had given us in our turn the right to be born American.*

"*And in a little while even our sons would forget, and the old-country people would be only a dimming memory, and names would mean nothing, and the melting would be done.*"

IN the long light of historical perspective, probably no civilization is proud of the manner in which it has treated its minority peoples. At best, nations must inevitably fall back upon the rationalization that those early times operated under a code that numbers and might make right.

Of anyone, the native Indian has the most long-lasting complaint of shabby treatment by his white conquerors. But the Indian, too, existed by right of conquest over other Indian tribes. Wars, killing, subjugation, and the wresting of lands from the enemy fill the pages of Indian history as surely as they do the black, yellow, and white men's histories.

Before the coming of the white man, the primitive Nevada Indian had lived for thousands of years along the shores of prehistoric lakes such as Pyramid Lake in the north and the rare rivers of the south. In the northern summers, they either went naked or fashioned garments out of sagebrush fibers or the skins of pelicans, and in the winters, they made robes of chain-linked rabbit skins. They subsisted on seeds and nuts and roots of wild plants and pinenut trees, fish from lakes and rivers, reptiles, and the flesh of rabbit. Their weapons were obsidian-tipped spears and the hand-flung dart known as the atlatl. Until the bow and arrow were developed, Indians stood little chance of killing such fleet game animals as deer and antelope.

At first, they were cave dwellers. In later times, they learned to make temporary dwellings out of reeds and sagebrush, tightly woven storage baskets lined with pitch, nets for fishing and rabbit drives, and boats made from tules that grew in the swamps. They became nomadic in a limited sense, venturing into the mountains in summer in search for game, and retreating to the warmer deserts to wait out the long winters.

The Indian greeted the first white men in what is now Nevada with friendliness and almost childlike awe. There are no recorded incidents of warfare with American and Canadian trappers or Mexican traders in the first contacts between white and Indian through the 1820s.

Though Indian documentation of early contacts with white men is rare, one revealing description was written by Sarah Winnemucca Hopkins, daughter of the Paiute chief Winnemucca. In later years, after her marriage to a U.S. army officer, this remarkable woman became one of the first Indians to lecture and write about Indian grievances. In her book, *Life Among The Piutes,* she wrote:

> I was a very small child when the first white people came into our country. They came like a lion, yes, like a roaring lion, and

have continued so ever since, and I have never forgotten their first coming. My people were scattered at that time over nearly all the territory now known as Nevada. My grandfather was chief of the entire Piute nation, and was camped near Humboldt Lake, with a small portion of his tribe, when a party traveling eastward from California was seen coming. When the news was brought to my grandfather, he asked what they looked like. When told that they had hair on their faces, and were white, he jumped and clasped his hands together, and cried aloud, "My white brothers, my long-looked-for white brothers have come at last!"

The first trouble that was to set the pattern of hostilities occurred in 1833 near the Humboldt Sink. Mountain man Joseph Walker, who had separated from the exploration party of U.S. Army Captain Benjamin Louis Eulalie de Bonneville, encountered what he claimed to be nearly a thousand hostile Indians. Walker's party struck quickly, killing fourteen of them. Later, the Indians claimed they had approached Walker's party out of curiosity and without menace. Whatever the case, the stage was set for nearly three decades of intermittent warfare and recrimination.

The westward wave of pioneers served only to heighten tensions. Disregarding claims by tribal families to ownership of land, lakes, and the vital pinenut groves that provided main sustenance for the northern Paiutes, settlers took over the most fertile valleys and cut down the pinenut groves for firewood. Indians retaliated by isolated violence—shooting of horses and mules and oxen on the pioneer wagon trails, stealing cattle from ranches, and massacring small parties.

The discovery of Comstock lode silver in 1859 was the end of Indian hopes of retaining their native dominions. They were relegated to uncertain reservations to thrive as best they could. Others became house servants or hangers-on begging for their existence on the fringes of the new mining towns. In a predominantly male white society, some Indian woman had the choice of selling their favors or being raped.

When, in 1860, two girl children were taken captive by prospectors at Williams's Station on the Carson River, the final spark was touched to the major confrontation that had been so long coming. Indians killed the prospectors and rescued the girl captives. News of the killings spread in two directions—one to the white population and the other to an Indian council of war being held at Pyramid Lake between Paiute, Shoshone, and Bannock chiefs from as far north as the Oregon border.

The news arrived at the Pyramid Lake council just as a young Paiute chief named Numaga was pleading for peace. Historian Myron Angel, who interviewed Paiute Indians in later years, recorded his eloquent plea:

> You would make war upon the whites. I ask you to pause and reflect. The white men are like the stars over your heads. You have wrongs, great wrongs, that rise up like those mountains before you. But can you, from the mountaintops, reach and blot out those stars? Your enemies are like the sands in the beds of your own rivers. When taken away they only give place for more to come and settle there. Could you defeat the whites of Nevada, from over the mountains in California would come to help them an army of white men that would cover your country like a blanket. What hope is there for the Pah-Ute? From where is to come your guns, your powder, your lead, your dried meats to live upon, and hay to feed your ponies with while you carry on this war? Your enemies have all of these things, more than they can use. They will come like the sand in a whirlwind and drive you from your homes. You will be forced among the barren rocks of the north, where your ponies will die; where you will see the women and old men starve, and listen to the cries of your children for food. I love my people; let them live; and when their spirits shall be called to the Great Camp in the southern sky, let their bones rest where their fathers were buried.

As Numaga finished, an Indian on a pony dashed into the gathering and told the chiefs of the killing of the prospectors at Williams's Station. Numaga gave up his effort towards peace. "There is no longer any use for counsel," he said. "We must prepare for war, for the soldiers will now come here to fight us."

In Carson City, a ragtail volunteer army of 105 men was hurriedly assembled under the command of Major William Ormsby. The volunteer army, already lacking military training, was further weakened by an attitude of brash confidence about "teaching the red devils a lesson." The assembled Indian warriors turned both lackings to their own advantage. When the volunteers penetrated the rocky terrain near Pyramid Lake, they were lured systematically into an ambush. Indians caught them between two flanking movements and poured a shower of arrows and bullets into their disorganized ranks. The volunteers who survived the ambush fled for their lives. Most of them, including Major Ormsby, were ridden down and killed. When the battle was over, seventy-six white men had met their death, and of those who managed to escape, most were wounded.

The Indian victory was short-lived, however. The news of what was to become known as the Pyramid Lake War was dispatched to California, bringing four companies of trained U.S. cavalry from California. They joined a volunteer force of more than 500 men from western Nevada. Together, they inflicted a major defeat upon the Indians, killing 160 of them in a single battle near Pyramid Lake. As Chief Numaga had predicted, his people were driven into nearly impassable mountains, there to linger in starvation and finally disband. Numaga sued for peace.

Though the peace treaty was meant to be enduring, there was really no way in which the idealistic Numaga could control the actions of independent bands of Paiute and Shoshone warriors. They continued to raid farms and isolated stations on the main travel routes.

A network of military posts was established by the federal government to protect the farms and stations and the continuing flow of fortune seekers. Indian troubles subsided, but it was not until 1878 that a degree of tranquility was reached. By then, reservation agreements were formalized and most Nevada Indian tribes finally abandoned their nomadic way of life. They became farmers on reservations, hangers-on in the vicinity of military outposts, and menials in the white settlements.

Nevada Indians have never been reservation dwellers in any substantial number. There are twenty-three Indian reservations in Nevada, but at most, only half of the Indian population has ever lived on them. Others have chosen to congregate on land set aside by the federal government in or near such towns as Reno, Carson City, Dresslerville, Lovelock, Winnemucca, Bat-

Charcoal kilns, Tybo

Manhattan

Ranch near Manhattan

Downtown Las Vegas

Virginia City

Resident, Manhattan

Ranch on the Truckee River

Post office, Silver Peak

Hoover Dam

Searching for mustangs, east of Dayton. Photo by J. Bruce Baumann, 1973.

Basque festival, Elko

Near McDermitt

Buckaroo, near Pyramid Lake

Branding longhorns, Fremont Valley

Hard-rock miner, Goldfield

Pyramid Lake

Cathedral Gorge

Jarbidge Wilderness Area

Kingston Canyon

tle Mountain, Elko, and Yerington. Still others, who have prospered through jobs and small businesses, live in white neighborhoods that were formerly off-limits to them.

Indian rights, even on legally constituted reservations, went through a long period of erosion at the hands of railroads, agricultural interests, and land speculators. Lakes, timber preserves, and potential farmland were lost to the Indians through political pressures brought to bear on governmental agencies. The history of the Nevada reservation Indian is one of broken treaties and arbitrary land seizures. In recent years, however, the reservations have become organized into self-governing entities capable of defending their rights in the courts.

As an example, the Pyramid Lake reservation today is locked in a three-way struggle with ranching and farming interests and the rapidly growing municipalities of Reno and Sparks. All three entities are dependent upon water from the Truckee River that flows from Lake Tahoe in the Sierra range and empties finally into Pyramid Lake. Before it gets there, it must flow through the metropolitan centers and undergo diversion to downstream agricultural land. The Pyramid Lake Indians are claiming water rights under old treaties, protesting that the level of the prehistoric lake is dropping as each year goes by, and that their fisheries are being endangered.

The keys to the new status of the Nevada Indian have been education and citizen involvement. Both have been a long time evolving. It was 1891 before the first vocational Indian school was founded at Stewart near Carson City. In 1924 Indians were finally granted full citizenship. And in 1932 the right of public school education was granted to Indian children.

Even so, Nevada's Indians were slow in taking advantage of schooling and citizenship. Until the 1930s, Indian children rarely went to school beyond the sixth grade, and most Indian adults did not take advantage of their voting rights as citizens.

All that has changed now. Nevada's Indians are organized as never before, Indian children receive their full measure of basic schooling, more and more of them are going on to university levels; arts and crafts stores are flourishing on reservations; and nearly forgotten traditions of song and dance are being revived.

At Pyramid Lake, some four hundred and fifty Paiute Indians live on the reservation, farming and ranching and working in construction to supplement their earnings. Their jade-green lake, twenty miles long and resembling a giant-sized mirage in a desert setting, has become a favorite boating and fishing area for the nearby metropolitan centers of Reno and Sparks. The tribal council charges fees for use of the lake and leases sites for construction of tourist motels, restaurants, and bars.

As for the Paiute Indians who control the Pyramid Lake reservation, they maintain one important vestige of their ages-old tradition. There is no right of private ownership of land even for tribal members. And the right to fish and hunt where they choose is shared by all. This old relationship between Indian and the land is what the property-oriented white man could never understand from the beginning.

Western history and literature for too long a time perpetuated the myth that the frontier was settled by the American-born Anglo-Saxon. It is only in recent years that historians have dispelled the myth and shown that the frontier West was indeed a potpourri of nationalities from Europe and Asia.

Nevada was a classic example of that potpourri. When Nevada achieved territorial status in 1861, nearly one-third of its population had come from foreign lands. In fact, by the time the decade was over, the percentage of foreign born had climbed to nearly half the population, or almost triple the percentage for any state in the Union.

They came from their homelands for myriad reasons—impending wars, religious persecution, restlessness, lure of adventure, and opportunity. The last reason was the main reason. Trapped by old-world economic caste systems that denied the opportunity to better one's station in life, most came in search of the one key to escape from unchanging station—money.

And they found it. Poverty-ridden in their old-world circumstance, they possessed in common the willingness to work at any job, no matter how demanding.

Chinese and Hindus labored at laying rails; Italians and Swiss burned charcoal for mine smelters, founded ranches and built dairy herds in the valleys near Reno; Cornishmen and Irish worked in the deep mines of the Comstock lode and other mining booms; French-Canadians were lumberjacks in the deep forests surrounding Lake Tahoe; and Germans in fertile Carson Valley farmed the produce that fed the Comstock lode. Later, Slavs and Greeks worked in the mines and smelters of Ruth and McGill in eastern Nevada, and Basques and Scots herded sheep in the deserts and mountains. Others drawn from the thirty-three nationalities that peopled Nevada became merchants, opened printing shops, worked as maids and waitresses in hotels and restaurants, or became itinerant laborers in mining and agriculture.

Landless for the most part in the countries of their birth, they shared a common passion for ownership of property. That, combined with the thriftiness that seemed to be inborn in them, was parlayed in the space of a few years into prosperous enterprises, many of which have lasted to the present day.

Though homesickness and loneliness were something else to be contended with in an alien land, the foreign-born compensated by forming social groups confined to their own nationalities, published newspapers in their native languages, and celebrated the holidays of their land of origin. During its heyday for example, Virginia City could count on a continuous round of celebrations ranging from the Chinese New Year to a Scottish gathering of clans to a Mexican Independence Day.

In a social structure where the American-born Anglo-Saxon usually formed the ruling class, all the foreign-born tasted discrimination in one form or another.

In the summer of 1879, Italians in the mountains of central Nevada were engaged in gathering wood to be converted to charcoal for the mining smelters in the boom camp of Eureka. A dispute over costs arose between the smelter operators and the "charcoal burners." The Eureka sheriff, claiming fear of violence by the charcoal burners, sent an armed posse into the mountains. In the one-sided conflict that followed, five Italians were killed. The posse emerged unscathed.

In eastern Nevada, the company towns surrounding the copper mines and mills were a microcosm of separated nationalities. The town of McGill in particular was sharply divided into segments for Greeks, Slavs, Italians, and Japanese. These nationalities formed the "cheap labor" work force for the copper operations. They were looked down upon by "Americans," who commanded higher wages and better positions. Discrimination was rampant, and incidents of violence between the "foreigners" and the "whites" were frequent. Time alone solved the problem of company towns in constant conflict. As the young of the immigrants grew up, they showed marked athletic abilities and provided the core of teams that brought statewide recognition to the company towns, thereby breaking down the racial barriers.

In both World Wars, the industrious Germans and their descendants, who had played a major part in developing Carson Valley in western Nevada into a rich farming and ranching region, were forced to bear the sting of criticism, even to the point of allegations that they were sending money to the German enemy.

On the open ranges of Nevada, the Basques with their free roaming bands were the cattlemen's common enemy. Though they had been early comers to Nevada in the years after the California gold rush, they began to emigrate from Europe in substantial numbers in the years after 1900. Vilified by politicians and newspapers aligned for the time being with the established cattle interests, they nevertheless refused to be run off what they considered to be free range. They fought back with a ferocity the cattlemen had never expected, even when outnumbered by marauding bands of buckaroos who shot their invaluable dogs, scattered their sheep, and took shots at the herders themselves.

But like the rest of Nevada's nationalities, the Basques were tenacious. In the classic immigrant pattern, they sent home passage money for brothers and nephews to help with the sheep, and sisters and nieces to work in the small Basque hotels. The small hotels, really boardinghouses, became gathering places where herders could rest in their off-times or between jobs, speak with their countrymen in a familiar language, meet their future wives, and keep alive the song and dance of their homeland in the Pyrenees Mountains between France and Spain. Out of the ambience of these little hotels was born the tradition of the Basque festivals held each year in such towns as Elko, Ely, Winnemucca, and Reno.

None of the minorities of Nevada were subjected to the indignities that befell the Chinese. Recruited first to lay the railroad tracks that were spanning the continent, they later became woodcutters, laundrymen, herb doctors, operators of tiny restaurants, and menials.

As much as color of skin, fear that the Chinese were taking over the economic underpinnings of small communities at the price of unemployment among white men led to the Yellow Peril movement. Chinese were literally driven out of one town after another, their possessions confiscated and their homes burned to the ground. When the purge reached the stage where it actually became formalized by legislative resolutions, most Chinese left Nevada and went to San Francisco's Chinatown, where they could be assured of a haven of reasonable safety. Others returned to their homeland. Only a handful remained to weather the storm and become respected citizens. Today, the Chinese of Nevada are prominent in professions and business circles, particularly in the Las Vegas area.

The black was a latecomer to Nevada. In the rich 1860s, Negroes numbered less than 50 out of the total population. Even by 1900 there were only 134 blacks in the entire state. The building of Hoover Dam and the World War II years brought the first major influx of blacks into Nevada. Most of them settled in an area called Westside Las Vegas, working for the most part as maids and groundsmen in the growing resort-hotel industry. By 1960 the black population numbered nearly 15,000, and by 1970 some 30,000 out of the state's half-million population.

With the enactment of the U.S. Civil Rights Act in 1964, the black began to emerge as both an economic and political force in Nevada. In 1971, the first black, Woodrow Wilson of Las Vegas, was elected to the Nevada legislature. His election marked the second time in Nevada history that a non-white was elected to the state's legislative body. And in 1974 Lilly Fong

of Las Vegas became the first Chinese-American to hold important public office when she was elected a regent of the University of Nevada system.

Three decades earlier, in 1938, Dewey Sampson of Reno had
become the first Indian legislator of his native state. His election
was an event of no mean proportions. More than a century had
passed since his forebears had welcomed the first white man to
Nevada.

12

Nevada: The Sin State

1931

"If you can't do it at home, go to Nevada."

"Reno is a modern amalgamation of Sodom, Gomorrah, and Hell."

"You cannot legislate morals into people, any more than you can legislate love into the hearts of some professed Christians. You can't stop gambling, so let's put it out in the open. Divorce is the only solution when marriages are unhappy. And if I had my way in this Prohibition year, I as mayor of Reno would place a barrel of whiskey on every corner, with a dipper, and a sign saying: 'Help yourself, but don't be a hog.' "

*O*F such were the arguments that raged when, in 1931, Nevada in a single coup assumed the dubious role of the "Peck's Bad Boy" of the forty-eight states. The occasion was the signing into law by Governor Fred Balzar of two startling pieces of legislation—one providing for easy divorce and other permitting casino gambling.

The hue and cry was directed at Nevada from all parts of the nation. It came in the form of denunciation from the pulpits, angry speeches in the Congress, and indignation from newspaper editors. If the intent of the moral outrage was to shame Nevada into the paths of righteousness, it failed. All that it accomplished was to make Nevadans defensive, and in the process, bolster an uncertain support within the state's borders for its libertarian laws.

The arguments from outside were understandably charged with emotion. No less colored were the rebuttals from inside the state. Politicians and newspaper editors, who had been divided before as to the wisdom of the two laws, became joined in defense of what they termed states' rights. The voice from the pulpits of Nevada became a wee one and remained that way for the decades to come. High-sounding phrases such as "guardian of the frontier tradition that made the West great" and "last stronghold of personal freedom" became well-worn clichés. And as for the rest of the nation, it could go hang for its hypocrisy.

In the shouting match that has existed almost to the present day, Nevada's motivations have been all but obscured by the emotion. But it is possible now to piece together how and why Nevada chose to become the most often damned of all the states.

There was, of course, a grain of truth in the argument of frontier tradition. No boom town of the early West was complete without its gambling halls and red-light district. But by the turn of the century, the towns that managed to endure came to be dominated by the respectable element, and casinos and houses of prostitution were either legislated out of existence or went underground.

Because it was then a depopulated state of no seeming importance, Nevada's hangovers of frontier days went largely ignored by national observers and local residents alike.

If one were to choose a date when Nevada consciously began playing with the idea of flaunting social convention on a national scale, it would have to be 1897.

Nevada then was in the full throes of depression. The exodus from Virginia City and other mining towns throughout the state was well-nigh complete. Faced with hard times and a decimating drop in tax revenues, the state looked to its agriculture potential for relief. But farms and ranches in those far-flung corners had suffered, too. The decline of mining and the collapse of boom towns had robbed them of their major markets for meat, hides, grain, vegetables, and fruit. A few short-lived mining strikes kept flickering hopes alive, but only temporarily. The state's future seemed bleak and hopeless.

Coincidentally, 1897 was a time in which the sport of prizefighting was in ill repute not only in the United States but in half a dozen European countries. Though prizefighting had made a transition from the bare-knuckle, fight-to-the-finish orgies of blood to padded gloves and Marquis of Queensbury rules, the antiboxing elements would not compromise their position. It became a matter of course for world-championship fights to be cancelled at the last moment in such established boxing centers as New York, Ohio, and Connecticut. In some states, participants and promoters alike actually risked felony convictions under the existing laws. Governors and mayors were caught between the economic benefits of a championship fight and the wrath of a small but vocal opposition. Consider this typical newspaper description of crowd reaction to a prizefight in New York City:

> The seven thousand spectators, including all classes of humanity, let out yells expressing fiendish delight. It was a throng of people who showed all of the brutal instincts of humanity, which some people of the better class have tried to think in recent years had changed since the days of savagery.

Nevada was still raw enough not to suffer such queasiness about the "manly art of self defense." Indeed, the old frontier institution of the toughest guy in town willing to take on all comers was to exist in many small towns until the 1940s. And in the accident that befell Nevada in 1897, any qualms that even its legislature may have felt went by the board. That accident was the eleventh-hour cancellation in San Francisco of a scheduled heavyweight-championship bout between titleholder Gentleman Jim Corbett and Australian challenger Bob Fitzsimmons.

Seizing a heaven-sent opportunity, the Nevada legislature quickly enacted a law legalizing prizefighting. Its reasons were obvious: Nevada desperately needed a boost in its economy; California was but a step away, and Corbett was the darling of the San Francisco Olympic Club set, with a huge and rabid following of fans; people would come by the thousands to spend money for sleeping, eating, and drinking; a goodly share of that money would serve as an infusion into the pinched bloodstream of the state.

The fight was scheduled for March 17, 1897, in the tiny capital of Carson City. It was no coincidence that March 17 was St. Patrick's Day and that Corbett was of Irish origin.

The preparations for the big event were tremendous. It was almost like the recent old days when nearby Virginia City was at its zenith, and Carson City was thronged with traffic passing through on its way to and from the Comstock. But this time, Carson City was the hub of activity. An arena capable of seating the thousands of spectators had to be built. Restaurants had to stockpile enough food to feed the mob. Saloons did likewise with enough booze to stagger an army. Hotels added on extra rooms, private homes set aside family rooms for tenants, and arrangements had to be made for special sleeping trains to the Central Pacific terminal in Reno, thirty miles away, and from there, transportation by every conceivable means to Carson City. Hordes of San Franciscans arrived on the scene to cheer on their favorite son, sportswriters came from all points of the compass, and the dwindling towns of western Nevada emptied out their male population for the trek to Carson City.

The fight was a success from every standpoint, especially financial. Carson City had never seen so many people congregated at one time within its limits, it had never had so much publicity, and everybody made money. (Incidentally, Fitzsimmons managed to weather Corbett's clever boxing style through 13 rounds, then knocked Corbett out in the 14th round with his famous solar-plexus punch. Which at least satisfied the local gentry, who had thought Corbett a little too aloof for their tastes and had taken the good-natured, freckle-faced Fitzsimmons to their hearts.)

The lesson learned from the Carson City experiment sank deeper than anyone anticipated. From that day on, other Nevada towns moved into the vacuum created by prizefighting's controversial status elsewhere. In 1905, then retired world-heavyweight champion Jim Jeffries consented to referee a championship fight in Reno between the two top contenders for the title, Marvin Hart and Jack Root. Reno garnered an even larger turnout than had Carson City for its first world-championship fight. (Hart stopped Root in 12 rounds.)

In the mining camps, the Carson City experiment took on embellishments. In 1900, major deposits of gold and silver ore were discovered in southwestern Nevada, and a rush reminiscent of the Comstock lode was on. The boom towns of Tonopah and Goldfield and a dozen miniature prototypes were born. Again, a wave of optimism swept the state, borne out by some of the richest gold ore in the annals of mining. Again, the classic cycle of fortune seekers, merchants, builders, engineers, bankers, and stock speculators repeated itself.

But this time the promoters and speculators were forced to come up with new schemes to keep investment money flourishing. The old ranks of potential stockholders who had suffered in the swindles of earlier times were predictably wary of Nevada mining stocks. The name of the game came to be that of keeping a boom town's existence before the public. Newspaper stories of gold and silver strikes actual and rumored were one device, but editors across the nation, singed once, were not about to be burned again.

However, a world-championship prizefight was legitimate news. So it was that in 1906, boom-camp promoters came up with the idea of staging a bout between a black man, Joe Gans, and a white man, Battling Nelson, for the lightweight championship of the world. The promoters were led by a flamboyant onetime cowboy and Klondike miner by the name of Tex Rickard. By this time, Rickard had turned his back on his former arduous ways of making a living by becoming a saloon keeper and gambler. His Great Northern saloon and gambling hall in Goldfield was the biggest and fanciest the new strike region could boast.

The mixing of the races in the fight ring proved to be a drawing card, even though Gans won on a foul. Gans proved himself in his own right by knocking out Kid Herman in nearby Tonopah. (And Tex Rickard, having found at last where his true talents lay, went on to bigger and better things, such as promoting the first "million-dollar gate" in New York City, a heavyweight-championship bout between challenger Jack Dempsey and champion Jess Willard. Dempsey won.)

Following on the heels of mixed-race fight successes in Goldfield and Tonopah, Reno was not long in capitalizing on another lesson learned. On July 4, 1910, it staged the most controversial of all the early-day prizefights in Nevada. Former heavyweight champion Jim Jeffries was talked into coming out of retirement to meet the first black heavyweight titleholder, Jack Johnson. This time, the crowds and the nation's sportswriters poured in en masse. Every hotel room in town was taken, and miles of special trains with sleeping cars lined the tracks. Betting activity was feverish, and the publicity redounding to Nevada reached the heights. The temper of the crowds surpassed excitement. It was downright dangerous, not only because Jack Johnson was a black, but because he had committed what was then regarded as a scandalous indiscretion. He was living openly at his training camp with a white wife.

As if all these ingredients were not enough to create a sensitive situation, Jack Johnson battered the ageing Jeffries into a helpless pulp, finally putting him out of his misery in the 15th round of a scheduled 45-round fight. Johnson's victory was so overwhelming that it dissipated the threatening postfight violence.

There were other Nevada prizefights in the ensuing years, but none surpassed the record 15,670 crowd that clawed its way in to see the Jeffries-Johnson encounter. Prizefighting was gaining in popular acceptance, and public demand had smothered the opposing voices. The success of big-time prizefighting in Nevada had contributed mightily to a national change of mind.

As it did in prizefighting, the factor of accident intervened again in Nevada's second attention-getting breach of social convention.

Actually, Nevada had had a liberal divorce law, with only a six-months waiting period, on the books since the early 1900s. But it had never attracted much attention until 1906. In that year, playboy Pennsylvania industrialist William Corey, president of U.S. Steel Corporation and one of the world's richest men, became a principal in a divorce action. When Corey's affair with a dancer named Mabelle Gilman made the tabloids, his wife, Laura, betook herself to Reno to file for a divorce. That act alone guaranteed front-page coverage, and when she won a $2-million settlement, it made for headlines. It also launched, with one interruption, Reno's reputation as a divorce center.

Not relishing the unfavorable publicity of an increasing divorce traffic in the several years that followed the Corey incident, reformist groups managed to pressure Governor Tasker Oddie and the legislature, in 1913, to extend the waiting period to one year. That prompted lawyers and businessmen alike to form their own lobby, and two years later, the waiting period was restored to six months.

The wisdom of the move, at least in the eyes of law and business, was proven out when silent-screen star Mary Pickford suddenly appeared on the Nevada scene in 1920 for a divorce that would clear the way for a marriage to film star Douglas Fairbanks. Publicity resulting from her lavish stay on a ranch in Genoa was absolute insurance that easy divorce was in Nevada to remain. Which indeed it was. In fact, Nevada in 1927 further reduced the waiting period to three months. And, of course, in 1931 it capped the bottle by reducing the waiting period to a mere six weeks.

Then began the parade of celebrities who were to establish Reno as the divorce capital of the world—Vanderbilts, DuPonts, Morgans, and so on. A Reno divorce became the fashionable thing, and for every famous name, there were a hundred imitators. Dude ranches where potential divorcees could be assured of privacy in western luxury, horseback rides into the Sierra mountains and the desert with honest-to-goodness bronzed cowboys as guides, black-tie affairs at exclusive country clubs, a whirl at backroom roulette tables, blackjack, and craps, were all part and parcel of an exotic package. The assurance of closed hearings before sympathetic judges, sealed divorce proceedings, and the all-embracing clause of mental cruelty as valid reason for divorce added up to the final inducement. The financial benefits to city, county, and state coffers did much to ease the pain of the denunciations from those nether regions outside Nevada.

Even so, it was simply not enough to keep an entire state alive. Legal prizefighting and quickie divorce brought prosperity to a few communities, indirectly benefitting the state treasury, and kept Nevada's name before the public. But a monopoly on such libertarian institutions was temporary at best.

Prizefighting was being legalized everywhere, and other states were beginning to compete in the area of liberal divorce laws. The impetus of the Tonopah-Goldfield mining district's gold and silver discoveries had waned, and Nevada's tenuous agricultural industry had been caught up in the farm crash that preceded the Great Depression.

The development of massive copper deposits in the Ely district of eastern Nevada provided some surcease. The town of Ely had come into existence as a gold-mining camp in 1868, but neither the value nor the size of its nearby gold strikes were enough to cause a boom. It maintained life mostly by the fact that the county seat had been moved there from nearby Hamilton, a rich boom camp that once had boasted twenty-five thousand residents, then died as quickly as it had flared.

The first discoveries of copper in the Ely region seemed doomed to failure because of problems of transportation and reduction of ore. Then mine developer Mark Requa, whose father had been a mining engineer on the Comstock, struck up a partnership with the Guggenheim worldwide copper combine. Jointly they built a reduction plant, established railroad connections, and plotted out company towns at neighboring McGill, Ruth, Veteran, and Kimberly. Though not as glamorous as gold and silver mining, copper production over the long run was actually to surpass in dollars the production of the Comstock lode. Over the short run, however, it could not be counted upon to relieve Nevada of its economic woes.

In 1932, the so-called King of Nevada, George Wingfield, closed his statewide chain of banks and lost his personal fortune in trying to keep ranchers and farmers afloat. Wingfield was a cowboy-gambler-grubstaker-mine owner who had made millions in the Tonopah-Goldfield strike. Unlike his predecessors of Comstock days, he had chosen to reinvest in his adopted state. He went broke, but at least he had earned his place in state history for that gesture alone.

Apart from prizefighting and divorce, legalized prostitution— which had existed in Nevada since the beginnings of Virginia City—helped some in the business of attracting tourists. But not all that much. It served more in cementing Reno's reputation as a "sin city" by providing grist for the critics' mill. That distinction had already become well entrenched in the 1920s, when word got out that Reno was a major center for laundering money stolen in the rash of bank robberies that was sweeping the nation.

The mechanics of the laundering operation were almost painfully simple. Hit-and-run robbers of the ilk of Baby Face Nelson and Alvin Karpis headed straight for Reno with their loot. There, they turned traceable greenbacks over to two enterprising businessmen, Bill Graham and Jim McKay, and received clean money in return, less, of course, a modest handling charge. The stolen money was then slipped onto gambling tables owned by Graham and McKay, there to be distributed and hopelessly diffused a greenback at a time to several hundred customers who happened to win a hand at cards or a roll of the dice or a spin of the roulette wheel.

One of the dubious legacies of Graham and McKay, before federal agents caught up with them, was the first prostitution venture on a supermarket scale. Located in Reno, it earned the joint appellations of The Stockade and The Bull Pen, deriving from its activities and its horseshoe-shaped interior with a high wooden fence in front. Each crib faced inward onto a circular walkway, and scantily clad prostitutes (in warm weather) reclined by open windows. The strolling shopper had ample time to view the wares before making his purchase.

Defended by city officials and liberal champions as a safeguard against rape and uncontrolled venereal disease, The Stockade was a great hit among the local male population, traveling salesmen, and California businessmen. But the economic benefits of legalized prostitution even on such a grand scale were negligible. There were not that many locals, salesmen were too peripatetic to be counted upon, and Californians were hard put to invent reasons for that many business trips to Reno. However, it had proven one thing: there were distinct possibilities in the area of unconventional approaches to attract visitors to Nevada.

In 1931, the factors of economic depression, experimentation with libertarian laws, and a dominant Nevada attitude of stubborn independence contributed to the decision of the legislature and Governor Balzar in legalizing casino gambling. Not that backroom gambling existed only in Nevada. Few American cities of any size could claim with forthrightness that gambling was not widespread under their very noses. But actually to legalize casino gambling was something no other state had dared to do. Its prospects for the future might be surprising.

When the deed was done, the immediate aftermath was one of disappointment. The backroom roulette wheels, chuck-a-luck, craps, and blackjack games for the most part remained where they were. A few establishments, such as the Bank Club in Reno, moved their games out into the front areas, but with such trepidation that they still posted guards at the door. In any case, there was little fanfare. And for good reason. The operators of gambling games were understandably suspicious of the new law. After all, gambling had been legalized once before, in 1869, and outlawed in 1910. These green-visored, old-line gamblers, who had too often been victims of the whims of politicians, were not anxious to tempt the wrath of reformers who might just change the politicians' minds again. Anyway, they had been making a perfectly good living in the privacy of their backrooms, and a gambler couldn't ask for a better break than that.

Even in Las Vegas, a railroad stop that had had an unexpected boom with the federal government's decision to build a dam on the Colorado River, the new law caused hardly a ripple. Entrenched Mormon elders still controlled the town, and they looked with disfavor at what the lawmakers had wrought in Carson City. There were few people in Las Vegas, old and new residents alike, who cared to cross swords with the stern Mormons.

A full five years after casino gambling had been legalized, it fell to a carnival barker and his son—both outsiders—to probe the possibilities in the state's new endeavor. The son, Harold Smith, opened a tiny casino in a forlorn building on Reno's main street. It bore the unassuming name of Harolds Club. Apart from the standard old-time games and a standup bar for men, its main attraction was mouse roulette, where customers bet their small change on what color or number a scampering rodent would choose to rest up from his running.

If that piece of carnival gimmickry accomplished nothing else, it at least drew new customers off the street—ordinary people who had never frequented gambling rooms before, including women. The onus of visiting a gambling casino was neatly dispelled by the rationale of watching those cute little mice at play. While the uninitiated were there, they also managed to plunk a few coins into ponderous old slot machines or the smaller new ones that were coming into fashion. The metallic ranks of slot machines increased, the little club prospered, and Harold Smith's canny father, Raymond I. Smith, decided it was worth coming to Reno. He came with more than his suitcase. He had an idea. Why not advertise gambling along the lines of Piggly-Wiggly-All-Over-The-World, a market chain of the time.

Old-line gamblers and Nevada officialdom held their collective breath at this violation of the unwritten code of no publicity. But, in the vernacular of the trade, it worked in spades.

The secret of why it did work lay in the subtle approach to the advertising of gambling. Enigmatic billboards began to appear at crossroads and along highways across the nation, eventually to make their appearance in a dozen foreign countries.

The billboards portrayed a covered wagon careening across desert terrain. Emblazoned on the canvas covering of the wagon, in a style reminiscent of pioneer days, was the slogan: HAROLDS CLUB OR BUST! Depending upon distance, a signpost recorded the number of miles to Harolds Club and Reno. The word "gambling" never appeared. It wasn't necessary. Human curiosity, word-of-mouth, and amused or scandalized items in the nation's newspapers took care of that.

Stimulated by the rising tide of tourism and the opening up of gambling to the average citizen, Harolds Club was soon counting its daily visitors by the thousands and then tens of thousands. Most of this was repeat traffic, but that technicality was not considered important in the club's advertising program. All that mattered was that no trip to Reno was complete without a visit to Harolds Club.

The biggest gamble of all had worked, the stigma of publicizing gambling was off, and the rush to Reno was on. In no time at all, neon-lighted casinos were flourishing along two main downtown streets, all conveniently located near the establishment that had shown the way and launched a new era in Nevada gambling.

The transition from gambling emporiums, known among gamblers as sawdust joints, to the hotel-casino concept and finally, the lavish resort-hotel complex was swift and inevitable. The first phase was accomplished merely by installing casinos in such existing landmark hotels as the Riverside and the Golden in Reno and the Commercial in Elko. It was, in fact, in the northeastern Nevada community of Elko that an imaginative son of an old-time family, Newt Crumley, booked the first of the celebrity entertainment acts that became the trademark of Nevada gambling.

To the astonishment of the budding industry, Crumley built a theater room and brought to remote Elko such nationally famous entertainers as Ted Lewis, Sophie Tucker, Paul Whiteman, and Chico Marx. The experiment was a resounding success, drawing people in hordes not only from Nevada but from such neighboring states as Idaho and Utah. From that day on, big-name entertainment has never been absent from the Nevada scene.

Because the Smiths and the Crumleys were reputable citizens, Nevada officialdom smiled at what portended to be the fruition of their expectations in legalizing casino gambling. The smile was to become a grim one, however, when a man with good visionary talents and a no-good background moved to Las Vegas. His formal name was Benjamin Siegel. It was to be a while before naïve Nevada learned that he was better known in certain circles as Bugsy Siegel, who as it turned out, was probably the most vicious hoodlum that New York City's Lower East Side had ever spawned. In a district that had produced a good share of America's major gangsters, that was going some.

13

The Day of the Hoodlum

"Bugsy was a psychopathic murderer. He had gotten away with so many gangland executions that he felt murder was legal, as long as it was done by him."

"Well, you know where he got the monicker of Bugsy. It was because he was nuts. But nobody, not even Lucky Luciano or Frank Costello, ever called him Bugsy to his face. They called him Benny."

"Benny was the vainest man I ever knew. He dressed like a million dollars, tailor-made suits, monogrammed shirts, hand-made shoes, you name it. He couldn't stand the slightest blemish on his face. He would run to the doctor if he had a hickey. So, it was very disturbing to me to see that newspaper picture of him sprawled back on a sofa with two big bullet holes in his face, and blood all over."

"Hell, he was the founder of Las Vegas. They should build him a statue and put a historical marker in front of the Flamingo Hotel."

"There's no big secret how the boys are getting it on in Las Vegas. Muscle."

"So this big hood, now respectable, comes to me and says, 'We'd like to help you with the financing for your new hotel.' I

said to him, 'The financing is fine. I don't need any help.' He says, 'Well, we know better, my friends and me.' So I asked him, 'Who are your friends?' And he says, 'None of your business. I come to offer you money.' And I asked, 'In exchange for what?' He's getting mad, so he says, 'What the hell do you think? For a piece of the action.' And I said, 'Thanks, but I can get along without you.' He says, 'All right, I'm taking off the gloves. I'm telling you we get a piece of this joint.' I said, 'And I'm telling you no.' And he says, 'We're taking it. This joint will never open if we don't.' And I said, 'Get out of here, you sonofabitch. And don't try anything. I'll be waiting for you.'

Well, they burned down my warehouse and tried to arrange a strike and threatened my life. But I opened this joint anyway, by the skin of my teeth. After that, they couldn't touch me anymore.''

"Fitz was just a gambler. He was never in the rackets. But the boys had done him a favor when he was in Detroit. When he set up shop in Reno and made a go of it, they decided to collect their due bill. They wanted in. Fitz said he wanted to stay clean. They wouldn't accept that, and that's why he got it.''

"It was only by accident that I found out. I was a university student then, and a part-time reporter for the Nevada State Journal in Reno. When I saw that first story, I remembered something my kid brother had told me. He was working at a golf course at Lake Tahoe, and he had been a little shaken up by the fact that one party of golfers were carrying pistols in their golf bags. Out of curiosity, he pored through crime magazines to find out who they were. He found one man's mug shot, 'Russian Louie' Strauss, reputedly a member of Murder, Inc.

"I went to Carson City and talked the sheriff into letting me see Strauss. He was a tall, thin man with a long face and dead eyes, but he was affable enough. Never having been in the presence of a real-life gangster, I was pretty apprehensive. But when I asked him if he were indeed Russian Louie, he admitted it right out, with unmistakable pride. He went further than that. He said he was related to Charlie Fischetti, who had taken over the action in Chicago when Al Capone went to Alcatraz. I *couldn't believe my ears, but I decided to press my luck. He told me that Harry Sherwood used to run the gambling ship* Lux *off of Los Angeles, and then started reeling off the names of some of the people who were at Tahoe Village with him. Like Abie ('The Trigger') Chapman, George ('The Professor') Kozloff, and Abe Barker. The names meant nothing to me, but they sure as hell made for good copy. To top it all off, Strauss admitted he had shot Sherwood, but in self-defense. Right then, I made an astounding discovery about gangsters. They weren't like their movie prototypes. You know, brilliant minds that had taken a wrong turn. And poker-faced and tight-lipped. What occurred to me was that gangsters weren't smart at all. They just did things nobody else would do."*

When, in 1942, Benjamin ("Bugsy") Siegel made his appearance in Las Vegas, wide-open Nevada did not know it was about to pay the penalty for a half-century of tolerance that had begun with the first legal prizefight in Carson City. The fact that it managed at all to survive the horrific events of the years to come is a miracle in itself.

Given the situation as it was then, there was really no way Nevada could have known. In a word, it was abysmally ignorant of the machinations of organized crime. The few gamblers who knew Siegel's background weren't talking, and the few who found out were either bought off or terrified into silence. And after the cycle had started, the benefits to the state seemed almost to outweigh the dangers. That debate, incidentally, is one that has never been resolved.

Siegel was an enigma. To the local gentry of Las Vegas, he was a handsome, wealthy, hard-driving man with a mind-dizzying vision: the world's first luxury resort hotel complete with landscaped grounds of instant greenery and imported palm trees, swimming pool, restaurants and bars, and a showroom—all geared around a gambling casino that would put Monte Carlo to shame. That he had chosen sun-baked and shabby Las Vegas in which to build this palace was enough to quell those nasty rumors that such a man could be associated in any way with the underworld, whatever that was.

What they would not know for a long time was that Bugsy Siegel was indeed associated with the underworld. In fact, he was on the board of directors. His colleagues included, among others, such notables as Lucky Luciano, Frank Costello, Lepke Buchalter, Vito Genovese, Longie Zwillman, and Al Capone. Recognizing Bugsy Siegel's powers of persuasion (he had risen to eminence as one of gangland's top executioners), his associates had sent him to solve an organizational problem among crime bosses in southern California. After prolonged discussions, some of them weighty enough to be fatal, the organizational problem was solved, and Siegel began to look for new horizons. He found them in Las Vegas.

It took nearly a year of feverish activity to build Bugsy Siegel's personal monolith, the "fabulous" Flamingo Hotel, which opened during the Christmas season of 1946. By that time, his nerves were worn to a frazzle, his projected cost of $1 million had risen to $6 million, and his psychopathic tendencies had taken control. When his associates in crime refused to bail him out, he made the mistake of threatening Lucky Luciano at a meeting in Havana, for which indiscretion he later received two bullets in the head and two in the chest at his girl friend's Beverly Hills mansion. His body was not even cold before his successors, three notorious hoodlums, assumed control of the Flamingo Hotel.

The garish publicity surrounding Siegel's assassination and his bloody background sent shock waves through the statehouse in Carson City. State officials suspected they had a tiger by the tail, but did not know how to handle it. They floundered in indecision while organized crime moved wholesale into the open territory of Las Vegas. Luxury resort hotels proliferated along what was to become the Strip, a stretch of highway on the main route to Los Angeles.

In one way or another, most of the hotels were owned by the underworld, but there was no getting at the truth of who really owned what. With their highly developed antennae for anticipating trouble, bosses of crime syndicates were already resorting to the device of placing reasonably "clean" puppets out in front. These jovial dispensers of good will and donations to charity were the only names that appeared on license applications. In many cases, even the front men did not know who owned the hotels.

Before the demise of Bugsy Siegel, a wary Governor Vail Pittman had moved ultimate licensing authority away from cities and counties to state government, under the auspices of the State Tax Commission. It was indicative of Nevada's mixed feelings about gambling, especially in light of what was happening in Las Vegas, that state government did not have a separate department to control the burgeoning new industry. Even further revealing was that taxes on gambling were funneled into the state's general fund, a subterfuge to disguise the fact that "tainted money" was supporting such high functions as education. But one thing was certain. The tax revenue from legalized gambling had made state government solvent.

It was not until 1955 that Governor Charles Russell's administration finally gave a somewhat negative official recognition to the new industry by creating a gambling control board empowered to investigate the backgrounds of applicants for licenses. The control board was responsible to the Nevada Tax Commission headed by Robbins Cahill, a state official who had already demonstrated an unyielding position against criminal infiltration into Nevada gambling.

This was what the crime syndicates had feared most. Through their lackeys, they mounted a campaign to strip the state board of its investigative powers and return sole licensing authority to the individual counties. The crime syndicates counted on two ploys: one was the outright buying of a few key legislators, and the other was Nevadans' traditional distaste for investigative bodies of any sort. The syndicates almost succeeded. A bill emasculating the powers of the state control board passed both houses of the legislature. Governor Russell promptly vetoed it. His veto was upheld by the slimmest of margins. If it had not been, the door would have been opened for federal government intervention and the probable death of legalized gambling.

What prompted Governor Russell to set aside the barrage of arguments about new-found prosperity for Nevada was a rash of underworld shootings and killings within the state, and the stunned discovery that organized crime was trying to infiltrate Reno and Lake Tahoe, right in the capitol's back yard.

In 1948, a shooting occurred at the Tahoe Village resort at Lake Tahoe. So unversed were both state governments and newspapers as to hoodlum identities that the first stories named the assailant as one L. M. Strauss and the victim as just plain Harry Sherwood. Strauss was arrested at a roadblock and jailed in Carson City. A full twenty-four-hour news cycle was to pass before the underworld affiliations of the participants and their henchmen were made known.

L. M. Strauss turned out to be Russian Louie, reputedly a member of Murder, Inc. Harry Sherwood was the former owner of the gambling ship *Lux,* which operated off southern California. And the various witnesses to the shooting included such underworld notables as Abie ("The Trigger") Chapman, George ("The Professor") Kozloff, and Abe Barker.

Later, when Sherwood died of his wounds, Russian Louie Strauss denied everything in court. The small-town district attorney who prosecuted him had never encountered Mafia-type witnesses before. Every man in the room where the shooting had occurred, including Chapman and Kozloff, denied seeing a gun in Russian Louie's hands or witnessing the actual shooting. The case was dismissed for lack of evidence.

Though he won the legal end of it, Russian Louie was not as lucky with the Mafia end. He had incurred the implacable wrath of the crime bosses for his crude performance, and worse, bringing attention to the fact that organized crime had its tentacles in Lake Tahoe. He moved to Las Vegas, and one night two friends dropped by to pick him up for a pleasure drive to Los Angeles. Russian Louie departed, but he did not arrive. He was never seen again. Rumor had it that he was "planted" in the desert that Las Vegas wags describe as the archeologists' puzzle of the future, since it amounts to an unformalized but quite extensive graveyard.

The dust had hardly settled when state government was again to be shaken to its core. In 1949, Reno gambling figure Lincoln Fitzgerald was cut down at night outside his Reno home by a double-barreled blast from a shotgun. He would have been torn in two except for the fact that the first shot almost severed his spine. He fell so swiftly that the second shot merely grazed the top of his head. The assailants were never seen, and Fitzgerald never talked. For years he lived in a steel cubicle above his Nevada Club in Reno. Now, he seems free to move. Either his enemies are dead or he has been forgiven.

A macabre aftermath of the execution of Russian Louie Strauss and the shooting of Lincoln Fitzgerald was the ringing down of the curtain on any future acts of gangland vengeance within Nevada. State officialdom was puzzled as to why, until word leaked through that the crime bosses had handed down an edict. It was, of all things, a purity code. Henceforth, there were to be no more killings within the borders of the state. Transgressors were to be lured to Chicago, New York City, Phoenix, Miami, or elsewhere removed from Nevada. Once they arrived, they could be considered fair game. The crime bosses' reasoning was logical. They did not want to kill the goose that laid the golden egg.

Organized crime had reason to be concerned. A U.S. Senate investigation under Estes Kefauver had held sensational hearings in Las Vegas. Underlying the investigation was the serious possibility that the Congress might eliminate legalized gambling in Nevada by taxing it out of business. It was a dire warning that was to hang over Nevada for many years to come.

Indeed, were it not for the efforts of U.S. Senator Patrick McCarran of Nevada, gambling in Nevada would have died then and there. As a result of the Kefauver investigation, a bill was introduced in the House Ways and Means Committee imposing a ten-percent tax on gross profits of gambling. If passed, this bill would automatically have closed every casino in the state.

Senator McCarran was ambivalent in his attitudes toward legalized gambling per se, and strongly opposed to Nevada's growing dependency upon gambling-tax revenue for its very existence. Yet, he set aside his personal convictions in his battle to defeat the taxation bill. In a private letter to a friend, he wrote:

It isn't a very laudable position for one to have to defend gambling. One doesn't feel very lofty when his feet are resting on the argument that gambling must prevail in the State that he represents. The rest of the world looks upon him with disdain even though every other State in the Union is harboring gambling in one form or another, illegally, of course, and even though the State that he defends and represents has legalized gambling, it doesn't take from the actuality in defending the thing in open forum, where men of all walks of life and all particular phase and religious bents are listening and laughing, condemning or ridiculing. But, when the gambling business is so involved in the economic structure of one's State, one must lay away pride and put on the hide of a rhinocerous and go to it.

Public indignation in Nevada had been spurred by one exposure after another in the nation's newspapers and magazines. Nevada officials were no longer in a mood to be tampered with, and have remained in that frame of mind since. The Gambling Control Board was reinforced by a trained investigator, former FBI agent William Sinnott, as its chief. Sinnott, who had had extensive experience combatting organized crime in New York and New Jersey, established tested methods of ferreting out true ownership of casinos. Governor Grant Sawyer refined the investigative and enforcement arms of the Gambling Control Board by creating a State Gaming Commission with what amounted to autonomous powers in the granting or denying of gambling licenses. Governor Paul Laxalt took the process one step further by urging a law change permitting corporate licensing of gambling operations in Nevada. His intent was to make legalized gambling more palatable by inducing respected corporations to participate.

A by-product of this move was to bring the gambling industry under the hard scrutiny of the U.S. Securities Exchange Commission, a further insurance against undesirable interests. In the 1970s, Governor Mike O'Callaghan strengthened these processes with a stern hand. Today, Nevada gambling is one of the most rigidly inspected industries in the United States.

The absolute right of state government to control issuance of gambling licenses was challenged as late as 1977. A Las Vegas gambler who had been refused a gambling license on grounds of an unsavory background claimed that his constitutional rights had been denied. He was met head-on by Nevada Gaming Commission chairman, Peter Echeverria, who said that constitutional rights did not apply. Echeverria was supported by the Nevada supreme court, which unanimously held that a gambling license in Nevada was a privilege and not a right. The court further held that gambling was not "a useful occupation," and that its governance fell within the so-called "states' rights" Tenth Amendment to the federal Constitution.

All these moves have been procedural. What is rarely mentioned is the fact that underlying the success of gambling control has been the innate incorruptibility of the individuals who govern gambling in Nevada. Since the formation of the Gambling Control Board, there has not been a breath of scandal attached to gambling-law enforcement in Nevada.

Another function of the Gambling Control Board was to curb casino cheating of customers. Trained undercover agents and reformed cardsharps made periodic rounds of casinos, posing as customers with a yen for gambling. A heavy fine or revocation of a license was the penalty invoked against cheating casinos. Surprisingly, agents found little evidence of cheating in the larger casinos. Common sense governed that. Few casinos of any size were inclined to risk losing a million-dollar business for a few hundred dollars to be gained by cheating. There were instances, of course, when casinos employed cheating dealers (called mechanics in the trade) to strip an oil-rich Texan of his bankroll. But this was rare, and became rarer still. After all, major casinos had volume gambling and inbuilt odds in their favor, and tables and slot machines were there to take in money, not dispense it. Agents found that most of the cheating was going on in the small towns, where a gambler with a table or two had little to lose if he were found out and his license revoked. But under constant scrutiny and penalty, even these marginal operators were effectively cleared out of Nevada gambling.

A far more dangerous activity of those casinos controlled by organized crime surfaced in the 1960s, though it had obviously been going on since Bugsy Siegel opened the doors to his fabulous Flamingo Hotel. This was the practice of "skimming," in which millions of dollars in casino income were never declared for tax purposes, but taken directly from casino counting-rooms by couriers to collection centers in Miami, Cleveland, Detroit, and New Jersey. From there, the money was funneled into such rackets as narcotics and white slavery.

Again, the threat of federal intervention reared its head. It was no secret that FBI chief, J. Edgar Hoover, had in his possession wiretapped conversations among Las Vegas hoodlums and actual films of couriers en route to their destinations with suitcases full of money. Newly elected Governor Paul Laxalt flew to Washington, D.C., and told Hoover that Nevada would undertake its own measures to curb the practice of skimming. Nevada did so, and Hoover's evidence was never submitted to any congressional committee that might take it upon itself to investigate Nevada gambling.

Chief among these curbing measures was the establishment by the Nevada Gaming Commission of exhaustive auditing controls that exist to this day. Through these audits, the commission can tell at a glance if there has been an unusual shift in a casino's win-and-loss ratio. In the event of such a shift, the casino owner must demonstrate that his loss is due to a run of bad luck or a business slump. In any case, the audit control is a nearly sure check on the possibility of unreported earnings.

A lesser-known function of the Gambling Control Board makes for a curious turnabout to the established myth about cheating casinos. Cheating in Nevada gambling exists, all right, but it is by the customer instead of the casino.

In the gambling industry, cheating customers are known as "crossroaders," and there are literally hundreds of them moving from one casino to another. They are ingenious at their profession, using sleight-of-hand, daubing high cards that pass through their hands with invisible paint that can only be seen through infrared glasses, substituting doctored dice onto crap tables, freezing slot-machine reels at jackpot with a magnet, using wigs and disguises and a dozen variations to all their methods.

Thus, the constant surveillance of gambling customers not only by casino security guards but by the state's gambling agents.

Today, gambling-stimulated tourism is the state's major industry. With its billion-dollar-plus income annually, it is indeed Nevada's economic lifeline. It accounts for fifty percent of the state's tax revenues and nearly seventy-five percent of its employment. Mining, agriculture, and industry cannot begin to approach this impact upon the state's economy.

Despite the volume of casino gambling, however, it is a little-known fact that Nevada still ranks fifth among all the states that derive revenue from gambling. Pari-mutuel and lottery gambling in four other states—New York, California, Florida, and Illinois—surpass Nevada in total gambling revenues.

In 1976, Gambling Control Board chief Phil Hannifan described industry regulation as a model arrived at through painful trial and error in the face of what once seemed insurmountable odds. "The old days of cops-and-robbers procedures are gone," he says.

> Now, gambling regulation is business-trained and business-oriented. We work with the FBI, IRS, the Securities Exchange Commission, Interstate Commerce Commission, and at times, the Federal Communications Commission. Of the top twenty gaming operations in the state, twelve are owned by public companies listed on various stock exchanges. With all that scrutiny, you have to believe that the hoodlum presence in Nevada is either gone or so minimal that it doesn't count for much.

But, of course, the coming of Howard Hughes to Las Vegas had something to do with that.

14

Las Vegas Story

"In its own way, Las Vegas epitomizes the pioneer spirit. It's the story of Virginia City all over again. You know, pie in the sky, gold in the ground, or at least gold in them thar tourists."

"Las Vegas has a scale of values like a slot machine."

"There are two sides to Las Vegas—recreational and residential. The residential is what the tourist never sees. Off the main drag, it's like a small town in Ohio."

"Listen, in this town, there are only two priorities—a buck and a lay. And they're interchangeable. I have no prejudices against either, but when they become the ruling passions in your life, you're in trouble."

"The Mormon church takes a position against liquor and gambling, but it is a peaceful coexistence. We have no quarrel with the gamblers. We let them live their lives and we live ours."

"This is one town that's never impressed by big names. We've seen them all. The president of the United States would have a hard time getting a crowd together here."

"You wonder how girls get into this business. I'll tell you how. When you lose your job and there's no money. You're having a drink to ease the pain, and some bartender tells you, 'It doesn't have to be, you know. You got good looks and the body to go

with it. *Just charge some new clothes and come on down to the Strip one night.' So you say to yourself, 'What the hell. Why not?' The first time is the hardest of all, but then the money starts rolling in, and pretty soon you're not only out of debt, but you've got expensive clothes and a neat car. Then it starts getting to you, unless you're a nymph by nature, which most of them are. It is rotten, utterly. Your score goes away satisfied and proud of himself, and all you get out of it is another nail in your coffin. You can't go back home again, because sure as hell you are going to run into someone who saw you in action. So you become a Las Vegan for keeps. Which is rotten, utterly.''*

"I for one was sorry to see the hoods go. They brought class and excitement to Las Vegas. Ever since Howard Hughes bought them all out (he had a thing against them, you know), Las Vegas has turned into a little old family gambling town run by corporate cats whose word isn't good for twenty-four hours. At least when a hood gave you his word, it stuck.''

"Corruption as a way of life has been removed. The philosophy of the payoff is gone. More sophisticated people and businesses are coming in every day.''

$\mathcal{L}$AS VEGANS are at once their famous town's most avid defenders and harshest critics. Nearly every resident seems to have a compulsion to comment on Las Vegas, and every resident certainly feels that it is his right. This is to be expected in a town that is almost totally inhabited by people from somewhere else. A little more than four decades ago, there were only 5,600 people in Las Vegas, and most of them were newcomers. That does not make for much of an old guard. Today, Las Vegas has a population of nearly 300,000, and it is still growing by leaps and bounds.

In the uninhabited deserts nearby, government installations have stimulated the growth and importance of Las Vegas and southern Nevada. The Atomic Energy Commission, renamed the Energy Research and Development Administration, has blocked off nearly a million acres of barren land. The open-air atomic blasts of post-World War II have been driven underground by protests of fallout from radioactive particles in the air. However, the ERDA's presence is still formidable. Some ten thousand people are employed at the Nevada Test Site, many of them professional scientists. In addition to developing weapons for national security, they are engaged in peaceful nuclear experiments, testing and perfecting of nuclear engines that power rockets and space craft, and biological research on effects of radiation on animal and plant life. And Nellis Air Force Base near Las Vegas is the largest training center for pilots in the United States. More than seven thousand people make up its military and civilian components.

Las Vegas has had a curious history of exodus. In earliest times, it was peopled by the stone-culture Anasazi Indians, probably an ancestor of the Pueblo Indians of the Southwest. They first lived in pit houses, dwellings that amounted to holes in the ground covered by mesquite and sagebrush. Later, they evolved into a culture that erected a pueblo with connecting adobe rooms piled one upon the other. They were agricultural Indians who learned the science of irrigation and raised crops of beans, squash, and cotton. They also mined salt and turquoise, which were traded with nomadic Southwest Indians.

Then must have come a time of war, because the Anasazi abandoned their Pueblo Grande and moved to the protection of the almost inaccessible cliffs that overlook Las Vegas Valley. From there, they simply disappeared, leaving behind them an anthropological mystery of why they had left and where they had gone.

The next upon the scene, in 1776, was Spanish missionary Father Francisco Garcés, who was seeking a shorter connecting route between missions in New Mexico and those in California. He and his party apparently lingered for a while at the unexpected springs and the surrounding meadows that gave Las Vegas its name. In 1826, trapper-explorer Jedediah Smith entered southern Nevada from Utah. Following the course of the

Colorado River, he traversed the tip of southern Nevada, but it is unrecorded that he made a detour to rest his party at the meadows that Father Francisco Garcés is said to have stumbled upon.

Jedediah Smith's mission was threefold: new beaver sources for the Rocky Mountain Fur Company, a direct route to markets for fur in California, and a search for the San Buenaventura River that legend said flowed through the Great Basin to the Pacific Ocean. In this latter venture, he was to join the ranks of other explorers who had searched in vain for a nonexistent river.

In the 1830s, Las Vegas was a regular resting stop for trader caravans along the Spanish Trail from Santa Fe, New Mexico, to the California missions. Then, in 1844, came mapmaker John Frémont, who described the gushing springs with his customary attention to detail.

The ever-colonizing Mormons were the next to arrive. Urged on by Brigham Young's dreams of a western dominion, Mormons extended their chain of colonies from eastern Nevada to southern Nevada. One was founded at Las Vegas in 1855, serving not only as a mission but a regular stop on the southern trail from Salt Lake City to California. A fort was erected by the Mormons as protection against the Paiute Indians for colonists and travelers alike. At the same time, the Mormons attempted to evangelize the Indians and teach them how to farm. This latter venture met with mixed success. Though some Indians were converted, they also indulged in the pastime of carrying off crops and stealing livestock.

The mission failed in 1857, even before Brigham Young recalled Mormon missionaries to Salt Lake City. After the threat of war with the federal government had passed, colonists returned to establish small missions and farms in the southern Nevada area surrounding Las Vegas. After their initial departure, the springs and meadows served for a time as a cavalry and infantry station known as Fort Baker. Later, they became the site of a ranch under private ownership.

The ranch was purchased in 1903 by the San Pedro, Los Angeles and Salt Lake Railroad as a division point and prospective townsite. Freighting became a big business, stimulated by gold and silver strikes at Tonopah and Goldfield and a dozen other boom towns in south central Nevada. Lots were sold, and Las Vegas moved quickly from tent-town status to a community of houses and stores.

Then, in 1910, Las Vegas's hopes for a permanent community were struck again by calamity. Flash floods generated by a torrential rainstorm washed out more than a hundred miles of track on the Nevada route to Salt Lake City. It took five months to repair the track. That, coupled with the boom-and-bust cycle of the nearby mining towns, caused an almost wholesale desertion of Las Vegas. It clung to life as a ramshackle railroad town with only a few hundred inhabitants made up of railroad employes, miners, and merchants doing most of their business with Mormon ranchers and farmers at those southern colonies that had proved to be more long lasting. The railroad that had been the cause of Las Vegas's founding was acquired by Union Pacific to serve as part of its transcontinental run.

The federal government's momentous decision to build Hoover Dam (once known as Boulder Dam) changed all that. In the depression year of 1931, workers poured into Las Vegas and its environs by the thousands, and Las Vegas was on its way. Its prosperity was buttressed by the construction of the industrial complex called Basic Magnesium, Inc., at nearby Henderson on the eve of American entry into World War II, and in the next year, by the location of the Army Air Corps gunnery school at what is now Nellis Air Force Base. A few gambling hotels and motels made their appearance, and then, of course, Bugsy Siegel with his Flamingo Hotel. Though it has had its ups and downs, there has been no stopping of Las Vegas since. Even the advent of billionaire Howard Hughes was, in the long-range picture, anticlimactic.

Because it piques the bizarre in their particular brand of humor, Las Vegans choose to believe this story about why Howard Hughes began his massive venture into Nevada gambling:

On a night in 1967, Howard Hughes was secretly borne on a stretcher to a Strip resort hotel called the Desert Inn. In typical Hughesian style, his aides booked the entire ninth floor so that his privacy would be inviolate during his convalescence. Hughes liked the setting so well that he stayed on and on. This caused serious problems for owner Moe Dalitz, who needed the luxurious rooms on the ninth floor for "high roller" guests who could be counted upon to drop many thousands of dollars on the gambling tables during their stay. Faced with eviction, Hughes solved the irritating impasse by making Dalitz an offer he couldn't refuse—$13 million in hard cash for the entire hotel. Just because he didn't feel like moving.

The fact of the matter is less dramatic but more in keeping with the pattern of Hughes's financial wizardry and penchant for new ventures. It was that Hughes had just sold his controlling interest in Trans World Airlines for $566 million. Before that half-billion-plus could be consumed by taxes, he had to reinvest the money quickly.

Hughes was no stranger to Las Vegas. During his playboy years, he had made many quiet visits to the gambling mecca in southern Nevada. It goes without saying that a man of his genius in money matters could see the possibilities for investment in a high-cash-flow industry. That the industry was still looked upon with disfavor by a good part of the nation bothered him not at all. In his varied career, the unexpected came to be regarded as the expected. He had tried his hand with remarkable success at everything from scientific and technological breakthroughs such as pressurized passenger planes, outsized helicopters, and communications satellites to motion pictures, cantilevered bras, and a plywood plane for ferrying troops into combat.

The timing and speed with which Howard Hughes moved into Nevada gambling also belie the local folklore. He could not have arrived in Las Vegas at a more opportune time. The town had been caught up by overbuilding, both in resort hotels and private construction. It was an open secret that several of the hotels were in dire financial straits. Huge construction, service, and supply bills were owing, and the possibility loomed large that some of the troubled hotels might have to close their doors, with devastating impact on the Las Vegas economy. Hughes solved all the problems by buying up five more hotels, even going so far as to pay their outstanding debts. In rapid succession, he acquired whole ownership of thè Sands, Frontier, Castaways, Silver Slipper, and the Landmark, of which the latter had failed even to open its doors. He also bought up $30 million of undeveloped land, the North Las Vegas Airport, an airline, and a television station. He expanded his empire northward to Reno, buying the gambling casino that had started it all—Harolds Club.

Fearing a monopoly situation, the state administration put a halt to further gambling acquisitions by Hughes, though William Harrah's operations in Reno and at Lake Tahoe and construction magnate Del Webb's holdings in Las Vegas and at Lake Tahoe were nearly as big. Hughes then turned his investment capital elsewhere, buying up $18 million in mining claims throughout the state, most of them abandoned workings. In this venture, Hughes may have bought a pig in a poke, the price of his being a recluse unwilling to inspect personally mine properties of doubtful value.

Howard Hughes also had an innovative impact behind the scenes in Nevada gambling. Discarding by stages the old adage that "it takes a gambler to run a gambling joint," Hughes replaced many of the standbys with trained business executives. Banking principles and computers were substituted for the *modus operandi* of tradition. Rates for hotel rooms and prices in restaurants, which before had been kept low as a lure for casino traffic, went up sharply with the goal in mind of self-sustaining room and restaurant operations. The wisdom of this move will be a long time proving out. Though the annual volume of visitors to Las Vegas has climbed past the nine-million figure, some Las Vegans feel that the increase would be substantially more under the old system of low-priced rooms and almost giveaway meals.

Apart from his ownership of major hotels, the involvement of Howard Hughes was to have another profound impact upon Nevada gambling. Respected chains such as Hilton Hotels and corporations like Metro-Goldwyn-Mayer, hesitant because of the hoodlum taint in Las Vegas, had their doubts dispelled by Hughes's arrival. They bought or erected some of the biggest resort hotels in the world. The MGM Grand, for example, contains over two thousand rooms. New hotels continue to go up, and nearly every existing hotel is doubling and tripling in size. MGM Grand, Hilton Hotels, and others have also branched out with mammoth operations in the building or planning stage in Reno. To the immense relief of Nevada officialdom and the general populace, a by-product of all this activity has been the phasing out of hoodlum interests on the Las Vegas scene.

Outwardly, however, it is business as usual along the Las Vegas Strip and in that dazzlingly lighted downtown casino area known as Glitter Gulch, described by the locals as the place where neon came to die.

Along the Strip, the resort-hotel marquees reveal why Las Vegas is called the Entertainment Capital of the World. At any given time, they proclaim the presence of Sammy Davis, Jr., Elvis Presley, Frank Sinatra, Tom Jones, Wayne Newton, Pearl Bailey, and Mitzi Gaynor. Add to this the long-standing Folies Bergere and the Lido, and imported Broadway musicals, and one can understand how Las Vegas's entertainment bill exceeds $100 million a year.

Big-name entertainment is yet another lure to casino traffic. Las Vegas proclaims that no other city in the world can offer such an array of talent in resort hotels within walking distance of each other. Unproclaimed, of course, is the fact that the experiment has paid off. The huge salaries that entertainers command does not compare with the money that tourists will spend in an exposed gambling environment.

The weekend traffic from southern California to Las Vegas is almost bumper to bumper—tourists come to tan themselves by day beside azure swimming pools and immerse themselves by night in an extravaganza of floor shows and bare-skinned cabaret acts and casino areas as long as football fields, with standing armies of slot machines, whirling roulette wheels, and a myriad display of card and dice tables. It is a dizzying kaleidoscope of sights and a stunning barrage to the senses. It is Las Vegas.

15

Nevada Now

I T is a paradox that Nevada—the seventh largest state in land area and the fourth smallest state in population—is suffering mightily from growing pains.

This fact is not so far-fetched as it seems. Of Nevada's 110,540 square miles, approximately 87 percent is owned by the federal government. Nevada's 600,000-plus population therefore lives in 13 percent of the land area of the state. Though there are movements to transfer federally-owned land to state or individual county ownership, that imbalance is likely to continue for quite a long time. In any such transfer, Nevada would lose millions of dollars a year in highway construction and upkeep support funds now apportioned to the state because of the very presence of federally owned lands.

Most of the state's population is centered in two metropolitan areas: Las Vegas, which includes North Las Vegas, Boulder City, and Henderson; and Reno, which includes its adjoining city of Sparks. With the exception of the capital at Carson City, the rest of the population is settled in or near a dozen small towns of less than 10,000 population. Unless growth moratoriums are imposed, the population of the Las Vegas metropolitan area could grow to one million and the Reno metropolitan area to a half-million in the next twenty years.

Though Reno is not exempt, the Las Vegas metropolitan area has been beset the hardest by so-called "big city" problems. A

121

high rate of crime caused for the most part by transients, traffic congestion, and air pollution are by-products of its tourism-oriented economy.

But the more long lasting problem of the Las Vegas metropolitan area is an impending shortage of water for its permanent residents. These residents are employed for the most part in resort hotels and casinos, nuclear testing and research at ERDA's Nevada Test Site, and the civilian component at Nellis Air Force Base. If projections go according to schedule, the area will be confronted by a serious water shortage by the turn of the century. Since the average annual rainfall is four inches, the solution must lie in developing new sources of water other than artesian wells or the region's decreed allotment from the Colorado River and its meandering 115-mile Lake Mead recreation reservoir.

Several plans have been explored to solve the water crisis. One is to import water from outlying valleys within a hundred-mile radius of Las Vegas. Another plan, far more difficult in achieving, calls for a thousand-mile aqueduct from the Columbia River in the Pacific Northwest to serve not only Nevada but other western states. Desalinization of water from the Pacific Ocean is yet another possibility. These latter are long-range and perhaps impossible solutions. For the interim, cutting down drastically on consumption of water will inevitably serve as the most feasible plan.

Even the importing of water from deep holes in the Amargosa Desert north of Las Vegas has run into obstacles. Conservationists are fighting to preserve the existence in these deep holes of one of the oldest living forms of life, the pupfish. Scientists say that the pupfish, which lives in water temperatures ranging from near freezing to a hundred degrees, may well hold the secret of life for man.

The confrontation between the demands of growth and conservation has resulted in another classic battle at Lake Tahoe in the Sierra to the north. The pristine, high-mountain lake, considered to be one of the most beautiful in the world, forms part of the boundary between California and Nevada. Twenty-two miles long and twelve miles wide, it has seventy-five miles of shoreline—most of it in private ownership. The remainder is under the control of federal and state governments.

The deeply forested mountains surrounding it are dotted with ski areas that draw as many as fifty thousand skiers on a single weekend. But this is not where the main trouble lies.

Conservation groups such as the League to Save Lake Tahoe claim that Tahoe's natural beauty is being ruined by development along its shorelines. Population of the Tahoe Basin has grown from some twelve thousand in 1960 to more than forty thousand in the 1970s, and tourism has reached a level of nearly twenty million visitors a year. Though skiing and summertime boating, swimming, and fishing activities account for many of the visitors, the bulk of the traffic is drawn to resort hotels and gambling casinos in a limited area within the Nevada boundary.

Conservationists are aiming the brunt of their criticism at the resort hotels and casinos, claiming that they are a blight on the landscape. On the other side of the argument, owners of high-rise hotels such as the eighteen-story Harrah's Tahoe, the fourteen-story Sahara Tahoe, and the eleven-story Harvey's Wagon Wheel argue otherwise. They maintain that high-rise hotels are more practical and esthetic than the sprawl of low-rise motels on the California side of the state line. And private developers on both sides of the line claim that tourism and ecology can live hand in hand.

Ultimately, the resolution of the no-growth and limited-growth arguments will probably be resolved by the Tahoe Regional Planning Agency, a bi-state compact between California and Nevada that has the final say on the future of Lake Tahoe.

The problems of increased population in the metropolitan areas and too many visitors have extended even into the huge public domain that makes up most of Nevada. Environmentalists say that the state's vaunted wealth of fish and wildlife is being depleted.

In the five-year period from 1959 to 1963, as many as 30,000 deer were killed annually by hunters from Nevada and neighboring California. Since then, the Nevada Fish and Game Commission has established hunting quotas that are more restrictive as each year passes. Today, the number of deer in the northern and eastern regions of Nevada is estimated at 122,000.

Even tighter controls have been imposed upon the hunting of antelope and bighorn sheep. Antelope herds numbered in the hundreds of thousands a century ago. Now, there are some 3,000 antelope remaining in western and northern Nevada refuges. In southern Nevada there are an estimated 4,500 bighorn sheep in a 1.5 million-acre refuge extending from Tonopah to Las Vegas Valley. They are a prime target for hunters, but the factors of limited quotas and arduous hunting in craggy peaks are keeping the bighorn herds nearly intact.

Mountain lions and coyotes, once considered predators that could be shot on sight, are now classified as "sport animals" protected by licensing restrictions for hunters. Smaller animals such as the bobcat, gray fox, raccoon, muskrat, beaver, and otter still abound in the mountain regions of Nevada. Game birds such as ducks, geese, chukar partridge, quail, and pheasant are still plentiful. And there are thirty different species of game fish in the rivers and lakes of Nevada. The most exotic of them is the cui-ui, a prehistoric fish whose only known habitat is Pyramid Lake.

Conservation efforts, both governmental and private, have come in the nick of time. Depletion of wildlife is now under control, and the perpetuation of wildlife seems assured in Nevada's vast wilderness.

Until recent years, the prospect of parents from other states sending their children to Nevada for higher education was remote. Nevada's reputation as a sin state conjured up images of students spending their spare time and money lounging over gambling tables or consorting with hoodlums and prostitutes.

Firsthand inspection through tourism and the mobile nature of today's university student have changed all that. Visitors have found that the backstreets of Reno and Las Vegas are as prim and proper as their own, or more so in an era of big-city crime. And their children have discovered that university life in Nevada is just like anywhere else, and probably more conservative than on most campuses.

These discoveries have given the state's only higher-education network, the University of Nevada system, a national and international flavor. The huge influx of new residents has added to that. The insular nature of campus life in times before, when an overwhelming majority of students were from Nevada, has disappeared. The university student in Nevada today is very well exposed to a cross-section of ideas and cultures.

For nearly a century, the only site of higher education in the state was the University of Nevada campus in Reno. In 1963, the rapid growth of Las Vegas prompted formal creation of another four-year institution, first called Nevada Southern University and finally, University of Nevada at Las Vegas. Since then, the University of Nevada system has enlarged its scope with the addition of a community college system. In the five years from its inception in 1971, this arm of the university system has seen a phenomenal growth. One of its by-products has been the resurgence of cultural and artistic endeavors in small communities. This has been augmented by the Nevada State Council on the Arts, which has stimulated tours by theater and dance groups throughout Nevada.

The two metropolitan centers of Reno and Las Vegas, of course, have never been lacking for cultural events. The Reno Little Theatre is one of the oldest in the nation in terms of continued existence. And the arrival of Nevada as an entertainment mecca has not been without its fringe benefits. Musicians and dancers from resort-hotel showrooms, form in their off-times the nucleus of chamber-music and dance groups in both Las Vegas and Reno.

Due in most part to its historic experiment in legalizing casino gambling, Nevada's economy is one of the soundest in the nation. Its stage budget reserve continues to mount as each year goes by, and it has managed to hold on to its "tax haven" status of no income or inheritance taxes.

This has come about without reliance on the luring of heavy industry to the state. That syndrome so common to western states was abandoned in Nevada a decade ago. Instead, the emphasis now is in attracting "clean" industry of a laboratory nature, such as electronic and scientific firms. Basic, Inc., at Henderson in southern Nevada remains the lone industrial complex of any size, housing such companies as American Potash and Chemical, Stauffer Chemical, Titanium Metals, and U.S. Lime.

Under the impetus of a "freeport" law enacted in 1949 by the state legislature, warehousing has become a substantial industry of the "clean" variety in metropolitan areas. Under the law, goods in transit are exempt from state taxes. As a result, the Reno area has become the leading distribution center in the western states for goods manufactured elsewhere and warehoused in Nevada.

The kind of mining that was Nevada's reason for existence in the first place is almost a thing of the past. Only a few old prospectors still haunt the deserts in search of fabulous strikes. Except for the Carlin Gold Mining Co. in northern Nevada—which is extracting low-grade ores in massive open-pit operations—the bulk of mining now is in nonprecious metals such as copper, lead, tungsten, and iron, and nonmetallics such as magnesite, gypsum, and barite.

Legalized gambling and its resulting tourism are still the bedrock of Nevada's economy. They are likely to remain so despite the flirtation of other states with the legalizing of casino gambling. Even if other states do take the step, Nevada has two huge advantages on its side—a forty-five-year head start in the complexities of gambling control and a billion-dollar-plus plant investment in resort hotels and casinos.

So it is with Nevada now, a land that explorers shunned in the beginning, a territory that, with the discovery of silver and gold, became a crossroads of humanity, a plundered state that "didn't deserve to be" when the fortune seekers departed, a desperate state that broke with moral convention to sustain its very existence, a rediscovered region of America in which economic soundness and quality of life have caused a rebirth that will be a long time ending.

16

Postscript

SOMETIMES on a winter's night when the wind moans through the high trees and snow spatters against the windowpanes, and lights are low and the rustling fire in the grate suffuses the room with a warm glow, and home becomes a cave against the storm and I think about Nevada, I find that my mind veers away from what is considered to be important. I think instead of elusive moments and little memories. Invariably, they have to do with the enduring essence of land and seasons.

I think of a soft northern desert that stretches from horizon to horizon without intrusion by man. In fact, there is not a single tree to impede my vision. The only movement is the stirring of the topmost tips of sagebrush in the breeze of late afternoon, and high above, the silent soaring of an eagle with his white tail feathers spread out in a fan.

I am following a barely perceptible path that once had been a pioneer wagon road. The ruts cut deep by iron rims of great wheels have not quite filled in, and the sagebrush between the wide-spaced ruts has still not grown back to its full height. Behind me and before me, it is still faintly lower than on either side of the wagon tracks. And I am amazed, because after all, a century and more has passed since those tracks were made in the wilderness.

I think of a forlorn log cabin in eastern Nevada, surrounded by miles upon miles of golden rabbit brush and wheat growing wild in the patches between. The cabin looks out upon a sweep of valley land between distant mountain ranges. Its walls are made of hand-hewn logs chinked with clay. Once the cabin had been solid as a fortress. But now the sod roof and the thin poles and framework of branches that supported it have tumbled down inside the thick walls. The wooden stoop outside the door sags to the ground. Once, I suppose, a settler sat upon this stoop at end of day to look out upon the long valley and the changing hues on the distant mountains. Why he settled so far from any neighbor is something I will never know, nor care to know. The fact that he did is sufficient for me.

I think of a sand dune rising starkly out of an alkali flat that once had been a sea bed. The sand dune thrusts up a thousand feet above the desert floor. Its contours are soft and sculptured by the singing desert wind, but its spine is razored sharp. From that spine, I can look out upon the alkali flats that are dazzling white in the noonday sun. Funnel-shaped dust devils that are like miniature tornadoes whirl across the desert flats as if bent upon a mission, to bring more sand to the improbable dune.

I think of another odd child of nature shaped by the wind in southern Nevada. The impression of blazing heat is so intensified by fiery-red rocks and cliffs that I feel I am wandering in an inferno. The wind has wrought strange things here, columns and pillars and spires and skeleton ribs of rock. One mountain is like a gallery of misshapen faces of giants. Indian petroglyphs abound on the walls of this fearful setting, and I can understand why.

I think of the little Mormon towns in fertile regions near this Valley of Fire. Tiny communities with wide streets and neat, unpretentious houses of white frame and adobe brick, and the church meetinghouse that is the heart of the town and the people. On the outskirts, Mormon farmers in rubber boots flood their grain fields and tend to dairy herds, the orderly routine of their lives not much changed since the days when Mormon colonists set down roots in the desert and created oases in impossible settings.

In contrast, my mind travels to a lush valley in western Nevada settled by Mormons and then Germans. Alpine peaks of the Sierra, with snow patches still lingering in deep crevices in midsummer, loom austerely over the valley. The green valley floor is dotted with Herefords, Holsteins, and Black Angus cattle. In the spring, newborn calves lie on the dewy grass and gather strength from the gentle sun. And in autumn, the orchards that surround the white farmhouses are blood-red against the gold of old cottonwoods and poplars.

On the other side of those towering peaks, in a long basin where evergreen forests grow thickly down to the white sand of shorelines, is Lake Tahoe. And I am reminded of Mark Twain's saying that the clear blue waters blended so with the blue sky overhead that a man in a boat had the sensation of floating in air.

I think of the snow-dusted spines of the Ruby Mountains in northeastern Nevada, where the streams rush down the ravines in icy torrents, and aspen-covered hillsides in autumn are like blinding bursts of gold among the green of fir and pine. And the tiny town at the Rubys' base, its houses concealed under a canopy of willow and cottonwood trees, has a secluded park in the very center of town, where people can come to picnic. There is a worn board imbedded between two trees in that park, and the ends of the board have grown into the trunks of the two trees. Every inch of the board is covered with initials and hearts. It has been a lovers' seat for a very long time.

I think of a dawn when I climbed high up on a hillside to watch a sheepcamp come to life. By the time I reached the rimrock, the eastern horizon was edged with silver. In the crystal morning air, the waking sounds of the sheep carried up to me clearly. I heard the clink of a washpan, the scuff of a boot on bare ground. I smelled the woodsmoke rising from the slender chimney of a cookwagon. The distant barking of a dog reached me, and when I turned, I saw a band of sheep streaming slowly out of a ravine. The first sunlight shone on their backs. And behind them, wooden staff in hand, moved the solitary figure of a sheepherder. The dust that obscured him was like the premonition of a time when sheepherders and their flocks will have disappeared from the ranges of Nevada.

I do not like to think of other things that are gone, victims of growth and progress and too many people. Old houses in Carson City and Reno, with gingerbread trim and square pillars and encircling porches with swings and rocking chairs from the time when people sat on porches and watched their neighbors stroll by. And in the valley between the two towns, a little semicircle of land tucked under the brow of a protecting hill. Once there was a white farmhouse with an orchard in front of it that must have yielded good fruit to generations of one family. A slope of hard-packed earth descended from the house to a weathered barn from which snow and rain and winds had beaten every speck of paint. The farmhouse, the orchard, and the barn are gone now, and only the memory remains.

But the seasons remain untouched by man. Autumn in Reno, when the evening sky is streaked with long, uncertain bands of red, and the dry, rich scent of first fallen leaves is almost painful in its sweetness. Lakes and ponds that gleam like hand mirrors in the dusk, so that the reflection of a golden Collie running along their banks is confused in the still water with the gold of drooping willows. Unperturbed, the ducks continue their whispered conversations, and sentinel geese look on stolidly while pausing for rest in their southward flight.

And then one night, I awaken and I know a clean wind has been blowing for hours, and the wind is bringing in the first snowstorm of winter. When it comes, there is an overwhelming silence, as if all sound has been caught between the softness of snow thick-fallen on the ground and the softness of still falling flakes overhead.

And after that, the cold. A time when my breath freezes in the air, snow squeaks underfoot, and frost-rimed trees become complicated cobwebs against the gray sky. The winter wind comes sighing across the snow, flowing into my face and sliding across my cheeks until I am encased in an icy mask.

And then the spring, when the rain falls down caressingly at first as if trying to reach the tender new green that is growing beneath the snow. But soon it begins to fall with determination, driving relentlessly down, drumming against roofs, splashing in the puddles, staining dark the trunks of trees and revealing the rich black earth for the first time since autumn.

When it is done, the blue of the sky is as fragile as porcelain. There are pale-green clusters of leaves on the trees and the first adventurous buds of pink and white everywhere. The desert wildflowers bloom quickly in a riot of color, as if knowing their lives will be short. In the mountains, the snow begins its long retreat to the highest peaks. The deer follow after, seeking the nurture of new green and nuzzling their dappled fawns into the protection of the deep forests, as they have done since the beginning.

When the deer have passed from desert to mountain, then I am sure that summer has returned to the land of Nevada.

Suggestions for Further Reading

Myron Angel, *History of Nevada* (Glendale, Calif.: Thompson and West, 1881).

Remains the single most valuable history of early times in Nevada. Thoroughly detailed but uneven in organization. Fine illustrations of architecture, and biographical sketches of prominent citizens, including pioneers. Republished by Howell-North of San Francisco in 1958.

Eleanore Bushnell, *The Nevada Constitution: Origin and Growth* (Reno: University of Nevada Press, 4th rev. ed., 1977).

Fine historical summary with emphasis on governmental evolvement in Nevada, including effects of legislative reapportionment. Sound political analysis.

J. Ross Browne, *A Peep at Washoe and Washoe Revisited* (Balboa Island, Calif.: Paisano Press, 1959).

Based on two visits to the Comstock mining area, included in western Nevada region called "Washoe." First visit during silver rush to Nevada, second visit in 1863. Graphic descriptions of life and activities on the Comstock. Book drawn from articles in *Harper's Monthly Magazine*.

Gloria Griffin Cline, *Exploring the Great Basin* (Norman: University of Oklahoma Press, 1963).

A comprehensive but readable summary of the travels of first explorers into the Great Basin—Spanish, Canadians, and Americans.

Sam Davis, *The History of Nevada* 2 vols. (Reno: Elms Publishing Co., 1913).

A multi-authored work with resulting uneven quality. Author's own writing and editing touch, however, make portions dealing with dramatic events a delight—imaginative and humorous.

Dan De Quille, *History of the Big Bonanza* (San Francisco: A. L. Bancroft & Co., 1876).

Probably the most accurate historical treatment of the birth and decline of Comstock mining. Written by Mark Twain's contemporary on the *Territorial Enterprise* in Virginia City.

Alfred Doten, *The Journals of Alfred Doten: 1849–1903,* edited by Walter Van Tilburg Clark, 3 vols. (Reno: University of Nevada Press, 1975).

Described by author Walter Van Tilburg Clark, editor of the journals, as the most revealing account of life in the California gold rush and the Nevada silver rush. Based on a daily diary kept for fifty-four years by a sometimes miner and newspaperman.

William A. Douglass and Jon Bilbao, *Amerikanuak: Basques in the New World* (Reno: University of Nevada Press, 1975).

Traces five centuries of Basque presence in the Americas, with particular emphasis on role of the Basques in the building of the western sheep industry.

Wells Drury, *An Editor on the Comstock Lode* (Palo Alto, Calif.: Pacific Books, 1948).

A contemporary of Mark Twain describes frontier newspapering in the Comstock mining boom. Highly readable and revealing.

Russell R. Elliott, *History of Nevada* (Lincoln: University of Nebraska Press, 1973).

By far the most comprehensive and accurate history written on Nevada, from geological formation of the land to present times. Mining booms, politics, and economics are emphasized. The definitive historical work on Nevada.

Russell R. Elliott, *Nevada's Twentieth-Century Mining Boom: Tonopah, Goldfield, Ely* (Reno: University of Nevada Press, 1966).

The first detailed work to center attention on the latter-day gold and silver booms and copper mining, overshadowed by the fame of the nineteenth century Comstock lode.

Jack D. Forbes, *The Nevada Indian Speaks* (Reno: University of Nevada Press, 1967).

Chronicles the Indians' long struggle for rights in Nevada. Drawn from rare Indian writings, reports of Indian agents, and records of meetings with white men.

John Charles Frémont, *Memoirs of My Life* (Chicago: Belford, Clarke and Co., 1887).

Frémont's own account of explorations from 1842 through 1854 in the West. Interesting in primary-source detail, but unobjective in opinion.

Clel Georgetta, *Golden Fleece in Nevada* (Reno: Venture Publishing Co., 1972).

Traces the sheep industry of Nevada from earliest times, including the building of empires. Outspoken views on federal government jurisdiction over lands. Includes biographies of sheep barons.

Mary Ellen Glass, *Silver and Politics in Nevada: 1892–1902* (Reno: University of Nevada Press, 1969).

The fluctuations of the world silver market, and the roles played by Nevada's political figures in silver conflicts. Soundly researched.

Sarah Winnemucca Hopkins, *Life Among the Piutes* (Boston: Putnam Publishers, 1883).

Valuable for its internal view of Indian life and personal nature of one of the first Indian women to speak out against treatment by white men.

James W. Hulse, *The Nevada Adventure* (Reno: University of Nevada Press, 3rd rev. ed., 1972).

Highly readable account of Nevada from prehistory to modern times. Written as high-school text, but commands adult attention.

Richard G. Lillard, *Desert Challenge: An Interpretation of Nevada* (New York: Knopf, 1942).

Much quoted treatment of Nevada's differences. Historical and interpretive, dealing with communities and lifestyles.

Effie Mona Mack, *Mark Twain in Nevada* (New York: Charles Scribner's Sons, 1947).

Delightful account of Mark Twain's adventures in Nevada during territorial days and first statehood. Includes Twain's brushes with political figures and beginnings as a Comstock newspaperman.

David Myrick, *Railroads of Nevada and Eastern California* (Berkeley, Calif.: Howell-North Books, 1962).

Authoritative source of the development of Nevada's railway system, particularly of shortline railroads that have disappeared.

Gilman M. Ostrander, *Nevada: The Great Rotten Borough, 1859–1964* (New York: Knopf, 1966).

Revealing of politics in the Comstock era particularly. Probably the most comprehensive work on Nevada political figures to 1964, but from external viewpoint.

Stanley W. Paher, *Nevada Ghost Towns and Mining Camps* (Berkeley, Calif: Howell-North Books, 1970).

Detailed history of vanished and existing mining camps. Contains numerous unpublished photographs.

Edna B. Patterson, Louise A. Ulph, and Victor Goodwin, *Nevada's Northeast Frontier* (Sparks: Western Printing & Publishing Co., 1969).

Reveals much field work in northeastern Nevada. Sound treatment of Indian history in the region. Emphasis on evolvement of area.

Wilbur S. Shepperson, *Restless Strangers: Nevada's Immigrants and Their Interpreters* (Reno: University of Nevada Press, 1970).

The first detailed work on Nevada's history as the largest foreign-born state. Drawn from census records, but illuminated highly by personal interviews with immigrants of Nevada. An evaluation of treatment by newspapermen and writers.

Wilbur S. Shepperson, *Retreat to Nevada: A Socialist Colony of World War I.* (Reno: University of Nevada Press, 1966).

The decline and fall of a utopian colony named Nevada City in the early twentieth century. Drawn from records, letters, and interviews.

William Morris Stewart, *The Reminiscences of Senator William M. Stewart* (New York: Neal Publishing Co., 1908).

Exaggerated to some degree, but revealing of the character and political record of Stewart. Humorous references in a Twainian style.

Margaret Wheat, *Survival Arts of the Primitive Paiutes* (Reno: University of Nevada Press, 1968).

Illustrated account of how Nevada's Indians survived before the coming of the white man. Firsthand accounts of harvesting seeds, making clothes and shelters.

Quoted material in this book is from the following sources:

p. 37   J. Ross Browne, "A Peep at Washoe and Washoe Revisited," *Harper's Monthly Magazine,* 22 (December, 1860).

p. 40   Hoffman Birney, *Zealots of Zion* (Philadelphia: Penn Publishing Co., 1931), p. 292.

p. 45   Samuel L. Clemens, *Mark Twain's Autobiography,* 2 vols. (New York: Harper & Brothers, 1924), 2:305.

p. 48   Clemens, *Mark Twain's Autobiography,* 2:305.

p. 52   Albert Bigelow Paine, *Mark Twain: A Biography,* 4 vols. (1912; New York, Harper & Brothers, 1935), p. 1247.

p. 54   Mark Twain, *Roughing It* (Hartford: American Publishing Co., 1871), p. 190.

pp. 60-61 Sam P. Davis, ed., *The History of Nevada* (Reno, Los Angeles: Elms Publishing Co., 1913), p. 255.

p. 78   Robert Laxalt, *Sweet Promised Land* (New York: Harper and Row, 1957), p. 66.

pp. 79-80 Sarah Winnemucca Hopkins, *Life Among the Piutes* (New York: G. P. Putnam's Sons, 1883), p. 5.

p. 81   Myron Angel, *History of Nevada* (Oakland, California: Thompson and West, 1881), pp. 150–152.

p. 91   "Jeffries The Winner" in the *New York Herald Tribune,* May 12, 1900.

p. 109 Senator Patrick McCarran to Norman Biltz, July 3, 1951. Reprinted by permission of Sister Margaret Patricia McCarran.

p. 112 Interview by author with Phil Hannifan.

Index